The Mystery, the Way, and the Journey

The Mystery, the Way, and the Journey

Walking into the Darkness of the Unknown

Joshua S. Hopping

Foreword by Ron Dart

WIPF & STOCK · Eugene, Oregon

THE MYSTERY, THE WAY, AND THE JOURNEY
Walking into the Darkness of the Unknown

Copyright © 2021 Joshua S. Hopping. All rights reserved. Except for brief quotations in critical publications or reviews, no part of this book may be reproduced in any manner without prior written permission from the publisher. Write: Permissions, Wipf and Stock Publishers, 199 W. 8th Ave., Suite 3, Eugene, OR 97401.

Wipf & Stock
An Imprint of Wipf and Stock Publishers
199 W. 8th Ave., Suite 3
Eugene, OR 97401

www.wipfandstock.com

PAPERBACK ISBN: 978-1-6667-0361-0
HARDCOVER ISBN: 978-1-6667-0362-7
EBOOK ISBN: 978-1-6667-0363-4

04/23/21

Scripture quotations marked ESV are taken from The Holy Bible, English Standard Version®, copyright © 2001 by Crossway, a publishing ministry of Good News Publishers. Used by permission. All rights reserved.

Scripture quotations marked MSG are taken from The Message, copyright © 1993, 2002, 2018 by Eugene H. Peterson. Used by permission of NavPress. Represented by Tyndale House Publishers. All rights reserved.

Scripture quotations marked NET are taken from the NET Bible®, copyright © 1996, 2019 by Biblical Studies Press, LLC. http://netbible.com All rights reserved.

Scripture quotations marked NIV are taken from the Holy Bible, New International Version®, NIV®, copyright © 1973, 1978, 1984, 2011 by Biblica, Inc®. Used by permission of Zondervan. All rights reserved worldwide. www.zondervan.com.

Scripture quotations marked NTfE are taken from The New Testament for Everyone, copyright © Nicholas Thomas Wright 2011. Used by permission of the Society for Promoting Christian Knowledge, London. All rights reserved.

Scripture quotations marked TLB are taken from The Living Bible, copyright © 1971. Used by permission of Tyndale House Publishers. All rights reserved.

"Do Not Go Gentle into That Good Night" by Dylan Thomas reproduced from *The Poems of Dylan Thomas*, copyright ©1952 by Dylan Thomas. Copyright holder: The Dylan Thomas Trust. Reprinted by permission of New Directions Publishing Corp (US and Canada permission).

Dedicated to the anonymous priest who took the time to chat with a stranger and left him with some books.

Contents

Foreword by Ron Dart | ix

1. The Act of Embracing | 1

Part 1: The Mystery | 9
   2. Loving the Unknowable | 11
   3. Through the Darkness | 24
   4. Beyond Knowing | 35

Part 2: The Way | 43
   5. Allegiance to the King | 45
   6. Salvation in Motion | 55
   7. Doing What Jesus Did | 62

Part 3: The Journey | 69
   8. On the Path | 71
   9. Dying in Color | 83
   10. Chasing the Wild Goose | 94

Acknowledgements | 105
About the Author | 109
Bibliography | 111

Foreword

The lyf so short, the craft so long to learne.
—GEOFFREY CHAUCER[1]

EACH GENERATION MUST, AGAIN and again, wrestle with the perennial tensions of knowing-unknowing, doubt-faith, contemplation-charity, positiva-cataphatic and negativa-apophatic ways of knowing God and self, and what such distinctions mean for the public good. Sadly so, such needful tensions are often ignored by lesser thinkers who either focus on absolute certainty on significant issues or reduce all things to a matter of perspective and sheer opinion. And, then there are the difficult and besetting dilemmas of God and violence in the Hebrew canon, penal-juridical theory of the atonement, and eternal punishment for those who have not accepted Christ in this our all too short and all too human journey through time.

There has been, in the last few decades, a growing restlessness and unease within the conservative evangelical tribe, with the excessive simplicity of how the faith journey is understood and interpreted, and the corresponding and addictive need for absolute certainty that is constrictive and suffocating. Many of the more curious, thoughtful, and creative people within such a small womb are feeling the birth pangs and emerging into a fuller vision of life—such is the maturing beauty of Joshua Hopping and many

1. Chaucer, *Parliament of Foules*, 51.

Foreword

like him and, equally significant, the focus of this timely and timeless portal and key in the ignition book.

The tragic fact most live with today is memoricide (a sheer lack of even minimal memory of the grandeur of the Christian tradition). Such a lack of memory means most are vulnerable to a variety of pied pipers that claim to speak for the Christian tradition. Memory is a form of intellectual self-defense against those who would selectively go cherry-picking with the fullness of mother lode of the faith vision. A mature and creative way to respond to a form of narrowness and thinness of faith is to sit and linger with men and woman who have both thought deeply and lived meaningfully their faith pilgrimage.

Joshua has, rightly so, entitled his MA theis (St. Stephen's University in New Brunswick), turned book, *The Mystery, the Way, and the Journey: Walking into the Darkness of the Unknown*. There are many women and men, *ammas* and *abbas* within the Christian tradition (East and West) that have pondered the perennial themes Joshua has focused on, but there can be no doubt Maximos the Confessor (580–662 CE) is a saint and sage of the highest quality. The wisdom gleaned from Maximos is a definite antidote and vaccine to the debilitating virus of a form of immature Christianity that leads to soul, mind, and imagination illnesses. Those who long for health can certainly learn much from Maximos, a faithful physician of the soul.

There is, indeed, an unfolding mystery about the faith journey and the way itself is often unclear and unsure. Those who offer religious bromides and formulas inevitably do much to discredit the often complex and ambiguous nature of how Christianity is to be thought and lived. And, as the subtitle of this bounty of a book discerningly and judiciously suggests, often much darkness is in the walking, much unknown and unclear. Those who claim to have absolute answers are often more guilty of taking God's name in vain and creating idols of their ideas than reflecting the mystery of God's just love in the midst of, often, much tragedy and human suffering.

Joshua has learned much from sitting at the feet of Maximos and, thoughtfully so, he has only mined a few of the shafts

Foreword

of Maximos' layered insights, *Philokalia* a superb mother lode of poignant insights. The *Philokalia*, for those unfamiliar with this treasure trove of Orthodox contemplative theology, brings together, in a congealed and spear point manner, the best and wisest of Orthodox Christianity, and, I might add, Maximos stands on the shoulders of those who went before him. It is quite fitting and appropriate, therefore, that Joshua should chose such a wise mentor and guide into the way of the mystery, such a pathway into the luminous darkness, a way of unknowing that is, equally so, a way of ever deeper wisdom and love, markings left behind by those who have trekked such a trail to finer vistas.

I began this short introduction with a quote from Geoffrey Chaucer. He was acutely aware of the deeper realities of meaningful transformation and deification that Maximos understood so wisely and well. There are three main sections in the book: (1) The Mystery, (2) The Way, and (3) The Journey. It is best when reading a good book to step beyond merely reading for information and allow the book to be a midwife of transformation. Certainly, Joshua's book can do this if read in the spirit in which it was written.

I highly recommend multiple meditative reads of this pure diamond of a book. I was Joshua's external reader for his well-wrought and finely textured MA thesis and, I expect, Joshua, as he hikes ever forward on the faith journey, has much yet to offer from his deeper dives in the larger ocean of the Christian tradition, Maximos and many other saints yet to appear to reveal much that has yet been concealed.

Amor Vincit Omnia

Ron Dart
Department of Political Studies/Philosophy/Religious Studies
University of the Fraser Valley
Abbotsford, British Columbia, Canada

— 1 —

The Act of Embracing

Let me discern your light, whether from afar or from the depths. Teach me to seek you, and as I seek you, show yourself to me, for I cannot seek you unless you show me how, and I will never find you unless you show yourself to me. Let me seek you by desiring you, and desire you by seeking you; let me find you by loving you, and love you in finding you.

—ST. ANSELM OF CANTERBURY[1]

MY RIBS HURT.

Fire spread along my rib cage, slowly moving towards my heart. It was a good type of fire, the kind that comes with being fully embraced by a pair of strong arms. Coupled with the fire was a sense of wonder as I didn't think a seven-year-old had that much strength. Yet somehow those small arms found the strength to squeeze the air out of my lungs and crush my ribs. And no matter the pain, I wouldn't trade that hug for anything in the world. I was being embraced by my son and it was good.

We might not think about it but being embraced requires something from us. We have to open ourselves up and allow

---

1. Anselm, *Proslogion*, 243.

someone else to enter our personal space. To be embraced is an act of trust. We have to trust that the person who is hugging us will not harm us but is giving us a loved-filled embrace that will leave both of us in a better place. In a similar way, choosing to embrace someone else requires faith and trust. We may be rejected and left looking like a fool, or we might get tricked with a knife wound to the back. Hence it is my belief that to embrace someone is a dangerous and risky action.

So why do we do it? We do it because of love. We embrace our spouses, our children, and our family because we want them to know that we care about them. It doesn't matter if the hug is short or long, hard or soft. Either way we are speaking a language of actions that goes beyond words. The same is true for those of us who hug acquaintances or strangers. We may not vocalize it, but we are telling each other and the world around us that love is worth the risk.

Embracing an idea or concept works in a similar manner. To embrace a concept is to bring it in close and to make it our own. There is risk involved in this action just like embracing another human being. The concept that we embrace may not have our best interest in mind or it may be just the thing we need to keep going. Either way, there is a certain amount of risk involved in the act of embracing something.

Embracing Jesus

Have you ever truly read the words of Jesus of Nazareth as recorded in the four Gospels (Matthew, Mark, Luke, and John)? If you have, then you know that Jesus' message is one of danger and fear. He challenged the status quo of everyone around him and invited people to embrace a new way of seeing the world. Instead of telling people to keep doing the same old thing, he told people to stop what they were doing and follow him. If we are honest with ourselves, the message of Jesus is one that we really don't want to embrace or follow. After all, who really wants to forgive their enemies (Matthew 5:44) or give all they have to the poor (Mark 10:17–27)?

The Act of Embracing

No, the message of Jesus is one of danger just as much as it is one of love. The carpenter from Galilee is asking us to trust him and embrace a new way of seeing the world. We are to deny our own desires, passions, and cares while embracing his desires, passions, and concerns. It is an act of supreme trust as we don't know if we are going to get hurt or not. This is why it takes faith to walk after Jesus, for we know not where the path is going to lead us until after we step out onto it. And when we throw caution to the wind and fully embrace Jesus, we discover something odd. Rather than finding a two-dimensional concept crafted out of the pages of a religious book, we find a real person.

Though it may sound strange, the way in which we see and process the world around us begins to change when we fully embrace the person of Jesus. At first it can be a bit disconcerting, but as the days go by, we begin to get used to the changes and start seeing Jesus more and more. He is there when we are talking to our spouse or when we play with our kids. He is there when we deliver that report to the boss or serve that cup of coffee to *that* customer. He is there when we finally set a hook in the fish that eluded us for so long or when we stroll through the trees listening as the land tells us the stories of a time long ago. Jesus is also there when we receive word that our grandparents have died or when our spouse informs us of a pending divorce. He is with us, holding us, and crying with us through the pains of life just as much, if not more so, than through the joys of life.

I know that this may sound like a cliché to some of you; after all it sounds a bit like the propaganda spilled out by those steeped in power and certainty. However, to embrace Jesus in the manner which I'm proposing is to embrace a living person who is full of mystery. Jesus is, after all, the Creator King who is both intimate with us on a personal level and at the same time beyond anything we can understand. As the late-nineteenth-century English poet Sir William Watson (1858–1935) reflected in his poem "The Unknown God," the Creator is at times too close for us to fully understand while at the same time seeming far away.

> The God I know of, I shall ne'er
> Know, though He dwells exceeding nigh.
> *'Raise thou the stone and find me there,*
> *Cleave thou the wood and there am I'.*
> Yet in my flesh his spirit doth flow
> Too near, too far for me to know.[2]

Do you remember that hug my son gave me, the one that hurt my ribs and set fire cascading through my body? That was a full-body hug that told me that my son loved, trusted, and fully accepted me for being me. He didn't know everything about me, my past, my desires, hopes, or future. He just knew that I am his father and that I love him. In the same way, we should embrace Jesus knowing that he loves us and wants what's best for us. We may not—or may never—know everything about Jesus or where he is taking us. But that is alright. It is enough to know that we are loved.

Embracing the Tension

Though this may be subjective, it seems that the culture in the United States is pulling people towards the extremes rather than towards the middle. This is true not only in politics or pop culture, but also in the church. We want black-and-white answers to our questions; to know without a shadow of a doubt that this is *this* and that is *that*. And while this observation may be slanted due to my point of view, I can't help but encourage you, my fair reader, to embrace the tension of life rather than the extreme. Live not so much in the middle as in between the pressures, embracing the tension that keeps us from falling off the edge one way or another.

The world around us is changing. Things that were once certain are no longer stable while those things that were rarely considered have become the norm. Questions abound where answers once lived. It does not matter what country or continent our bodies physically reside in; the time in which we live is a strange one. Buried deep beneath the noise and siren calls of the world there

---

2. Watson, *Poems*, 132.

The Act of Embracing

is a quiet but sure sound that resonates throughout creation. It is the sound of the Breath of Life calling out to us, encouraging us to embrace the tension of the unknown.

Rather than fighting against the wind, we are to throw ourselves into the storms of life and trust the embrace of the Original Breath that gave life to us. Though it may seem fruitless and dangerous to trust the swirling wind of a storm, we can rest assured that deep within each particle is a cross-shaped foundation that holds together all that is seen and unseen. Hence to embrace the Wind is to embrace the Living Lord of all of creation and trust that he will bring us safely to harbor. Strangely enough, when we do this, we find joy and peace in the tension of the unknown, between knowing and not knowing, between life and death.

An Intertwined Trinity

By drawing on the writings of the ancient church, it is my hope to introduce you, my fair reader, to this strange, yet old, world of tensions and unknowns. While it may sound crazy, I firmly believe that entering the Wind of the Living Light with humility and open arms will result in us discovering a way forward through the unknowns of life. We do this by embracing three underlying concepts that will shift the way in which we see the Creator King and the world around us. The first concept is that of the Mystery. That is to say, we must embrace the tension of knowing and not knowing. It is a worldview that is comfortable with unanswered questions, the grays of life, and complex issues with no simple answers.

To embrace the Mystery is not to say that there isn't a Creator or a savior. Rather it is recognizing that God is God and we are but humans in search of that which we do not know. The Mystery is nothing more than Jesus of Nazareth, the Creator made flesh. In humbly laying down our right to be right, we pick up the cross of Jesus and walk down the path of those who have gone before us. We who live today are not the first to embrace the Mystery nor the first to toss ourselves on the mercy of the Wind of the Ancient One. We move forward into the darkness of the unknown, holding

The Mystery, the Way, and the Journey

the hand of our Lover while being cheered on by those who watch from beyond the grave.

Coupled with the concept of the Mystery is that of the Way. For years the predominate view of Christianity has taught us that following Jesus is centered on a single salvation prayer that saves the soul from eternal separation from God. While there is truth in this view, I propose that following Jesus is more than just a single prayer. Rather it is a way of life that transforms our spirit, body, and soul along with our relationships, desires, passions, and, quite frankly, our life. To embrace the Way is to understand that our devotion belongs not to a country, concept, tribe, or philosophy. Rather we, the followers of Jesus, are exiles in our lands, walking forward through the unknown towards a future home where we will find rest in the arms of our Beloved. The tension of the Way is therefore knowing that our salvation is one of motion, moving toward Jesus with each step we take.

The Journey is the third and last intertwined concept in this trinity of ideas. To embrace the Journey is to realize that though we walk the same path, the experience of each follower of Jesus is different. It is a paradox of sorts in which we spur each other along while only catching glimpses of each other's Journey. Common to each of us, though, is the requirement to die to ourselves. We cannot walk the path of the Journey without giving up all that we are and throwing ourselves upon the altar of the cross, trusting that the Wind of Christ will carry us forth into that new world promised to us from beginning of time.

Interwoven together, the concepts of the Mystery, the Way, and the Journey paint a picture that will help us embrace the tensions of life while passionately following Jesus into darkness of the unknown by embracing the mystery of uncertainty as a way of life in which each person's journey is different. These are not new concepts, but old and well-traveled ones laid out before us by the mothers and fathers of the ancient church. It is our world of certainty and newness that is but an infant on the stage of creation. Though there are many guides from the annals of history that could lead us safely through the murky darkness of these three intertwined concepts, I have chosen to follow the example of St. Maximos the Confessor (580–662) due to his impact on the development of the faith as well as his connection to the ancient church before the Great Schism of 1054, which fractured the church.[3]

Knowing that we are not the first people to ask questions about the unknown will help us all move forward into the unknown knowing we are in good company. Just like the Sprit has guided those who have gone before us, we can rest assured that the Creator is in our midst guiding us though the way be murky and dark. Hence it is my hope that all that read these pages will lean in and receive an embrace from these strange albeit old ideas. And to that end, I wish to begin this time with a fourteenth-century prayer that graced the pages of another text about going into the unknown:

> O God unto whom all hearts lie open
> unto whom desire is eloquent
> and from whom no secret thing is hidden;
> purify the thoughts of my heart
> by the outpouring of your Spirit
> that I may love you with a perfect love
> and praise you as you deserve. Amen.[4]

---

3. Though St. Maximos will be our guide while exploring the intertwined concepts of the Mystery, the Way, and the Journey, I want to acknowledge the complexity of St. Maximos himself. It could be argued that no theologian wrote so powerfully or deeply on the human will (gnomic and natural) or on how Christ heals the human will through surrender to his Father in Gethsemane. Ninety-one letters and treatises have been attributed to St. Maximos with numerous secondary works focusing on his writings and theology. Since this book is too short to cover the range of St. Maximos's life and writings, I have chosen to focus on three of the four works of St. Maximos that appear within *The Philokalia* due to the influence of this collection across multiple countries and time periods. These works are as follows: (1) *Four Hundred Texts on Love* is a collection of aphorisms on the spiritual life. (2) *Two Hundred Texts on Theology and the Incarnation Dispensation of the Son of God* draws from concepts taken from Origen, Evagrius, and St. Dionysios the Areopagite. (3) *Various Texts on Theology, the Divine Economy, and Virtue and Vice*; though this text is sometimes taken as a continuation of the previous work, the content seems to be fairly distinct as a stand-alone work.

4. Johnston, *Cloud of Unknowing*, 43.

PART 1

The Mystery

Imagine a sheer, steep crag, with a projecting edge at the top. Now imagine what a person would probably feel if he put his foot on the edge of this precipice and, looking down into the chasm below, saw no solid footing nor anything to hold on to.

This is what I think the soul experiences when it goes beyond its footing in material things, in its quest for that which has no dimension, and which exists from all eternity. For here there is nothing it can take hold of, neither place nor time, neither measure nor anything else; our minds cannot approach it.

And thus the soul, slipping at every point from what cannot be grasped, becomes dizzy and perplexed and returns once again to what is connatural to it, content now to know merely this about the Transcendent, that it is completely different from the nature of the things that the soul knows.

—ST. GREGORY OF NYSSA[1]

---

1. Gregory of Nyssa, *Homilies on Ecclesiastes*, quoted in Ware, *Orthodox Way*, 23–24.

— 2 —

Loving the Unknowable

Hope is not dependent on peace in the land, justice in the world, and success in the business. Hope is willing to leave unanswered questions unanswered and unknown futures unknown. Hope makes you see God's guiding hand not only in the gentle and pleasant moments but also in the shadows of disappointment and darkness.

—HENRI NOUWEN[1]

NATURE ABHORS THE UNSOLVED.

Or at least it seems that way sometimes. To look around the world today is to see explanations for almost everything. How does rain form? Google it. What makes a rainbow colorful? Look it up. How does the universe work? Check out the newest data about cosmic background waves. How do people react in crowds? Ask a sociologist. And the list goes on.

The trend continues with books, games, movies, and television shows of all types providing answers to unsolved questions. Quite frankly we humans like to know what happened. If there was a crime or a murder, we want to know who did it. If there was an accident, we want to know what led up to the accident and how

---

1. Nouwen, *Turn My Mourning*, 60.

we can stop it from happening again. And if we don't know the answer, we will typically make up an answer.

A look back through history shows that humanity has always had the tendency to provide answers to the unknown. Some of our ancestors looked for spiritual reasons to explain physical events. Gods, goddesses, or the spirits of the trees and animals were behind each movement of nature and, in some part, the movement of humanity and nations. Others felt that the events (positive and negative) around us were the results choices we made in this life or perhaps in a previous life. Lately we have taken to explaining things through more neutral tones: atoms, quantum particles, shifts in climate, etc.

In a lot of ways this desire to know and explain everything is good. Humanity's desire to understand the world around us led to the development of central heating and cooling, computers, cellular phones, and the like. Diseases that once destroyed entire towns are now cured with a quick trip to the local doctor's office. And the list of awesome improvements goes on as engineers, scientists, mathematicians, and inventors continue to push the boundaries of what we know and don't know.

Yet, has anyone stopped to think about the cost of all this searching? I'm not talking about a financial cost, but rather about the cost to ourselves. What price have we humans paid in exchange for knowledge? What price have our nonhuman relatives (e.g., the land, animals, plants) paid for our searching? And has it been worth it? I know these are abstract questions that may not have a solid answer. And that is alright because in a lot of ways we win by simply asking the questions.

The Oddity of Questions

There is something odd about questions. The simple act of forming a question causes us to rethink the world. It forces us to put into words that which doesn't seem right to us. Asking a question is giving life to that nagging feeling in the back of your head. Once it has been asked—whether verbally or silently in one's own mind—that

Loving the Unknowable

question takes on a life of its own. No longer is it a silent concept bouncing around in the background of one's life. Now it is a fly buzzing around in front of you, causing you to stop what you are doing and pay attention to the issue of its choice.

Answers, on the other hand, are things of finality. Once an answer has been given, the question is laid to rest, no longer able to move around like it once did. You might even say that answers are made of lead as they tend to crush all that they touch. It doesn't really matter what the answer is; whether it is a "right" or a "wrong" answer. Truth really doesn't matter to an answer. No, the only thing that matters to an answer is that the question fly has been swatted and thrown into the trash as if it never was there.

The problem is that some flies are hard to kill. Rather than going softly into the night beyond, they arise from the darkness when least expected. Those questions are the hard ones. They are the ones that force the world to dance to their tune. They are the questions of questions. The ones that have no answer and, as such, become an answer in and of themselves.

When this happens, you know that you have stumbled upon something worthy of pursuing. It may sound strange in a society of answers, but not knowing can actually do more to free your soul than all the answers in the world. Learning to be comfortable with unanswered questions means living a life of trust. We trust Jesus with our concerns and questions. We trust the Holy Spirit to guide and direct ourselves and those around us. We trust the Father with the future and what might or might not happen.

I understand that this might scare some of you as you are unsure if you can trust Jesus, the Spirit, or God the Father. You have been hurt one too many times. I hear you as I've been there myself. Sometimes it is hard to trust the Creator. And that is okay. Part of being comfortable with questions is embracing the doubt that comes with unanswered questions. Though I've heard otherwise, I firmly believe that God isn't afraid of our doubts or questions. I can see Joseph the son of Jacob sitting in prison wondering if he really had a vision of folks bowing down to him (Genesis 37–40). I can see the prophet Jeremiah sitting in the mud at the bottom of the well with his knees up to his chest while waves of emotions swept over him (Jeremiah 38:1–6).

Doubt and questions are common to all humans. Rather than denying that we have such emotions, I believe we should embrace them. Let's own them and be real with ourselves and those around us. When we do that, when we speak them out . . . well, that is when we find freedom as we find that there are others around us with the same questions and doubts. We are not alone; there are others walking this path with us, before us, and after us. Together we can follow the words of Jude, the half-brother of Jesus, in being "merciful to those who doubt" while building ourselves up in our faith by praying in the Holy Spirit and remembering the stories of old (Jude 20–23, NIV).

Joseph, for example, eventually was released from prison with his dream coming true (Genesis 41–42). Jeremiah was pulled out from the well by those who believed and trusted him (Jeremiah 38:7–13). Perhaps this is why the Scriptures tell us to continue in our fellowship with others even though it may be painful (Hebrews 10:23–25). We need each other to remind ourselves of the faithfulness of Jesus throughout the ages. We need to tell the stories of how Jesus moved through his people in spite of their doubts and unanswered questions.

The Tension of the Mystery

In the years following the life, death, resurrection, and ascension of Jesus of Nazareth, the early church knew that the Creator God had done something amazingly different in and through Jesus. Writing a few decades after Jesus' ascension, St. Paul the Apostle would declare that the "mystery of God" (Colossians 2:2, NIV) that was hidden for so long had been now been revealed in and through Christ Jesus. Hence theologians like George Eldon Ladd can say that the "Biblical idea of mystery [is] something which has been kept secret through times eternal but is now disclosed."[2] Though

---

2. Ladd, *Gospel of the Kingdom*, 52.

this is true in one sense of the word, the term "mystery" has a complex history—biblically, historically, and theologically. Though common usage in English typically defines the term as "something not understood" or "profound, inexplicable,"[3] the word "mystery" has multiple other meanings depending on the context.

The Old Testament usage of the word differs, for example, from the Gospels or Pauline usage within the New Testament. The term becomes even more complex when one considers the usage of the word by different people and movements throughout history.[4] Because of the complexity surrounding the term "mystery," it is necessary to limit the focus of the word for our time together. Accordingly, I will be using the term "mystery" as defined by Bishop Kallistos Ware of the Eastern Orthodox Church in his book *The Orthodox Way*:

> In the proper religious sense of the term, "mystery" signified not only hiddenness but disclosure . . . in the Christian context, we do not mean by a "mystery" merely that which is baffling and mysterious, an enigma or insoluble problem. A mystery is, on the contrary, something that is *revealed* for our understanding, but which we never understand *exhaustively* because it leads into the depth or darkness of God. The eyes are closed—but they are also open. Thus, in speaking about God as mystery, we are brought to our second "pole." God is hidden from us but is also revealed to us: revealed as person and as love.[5]

The tension of the latter definition of mystery can be seen in the writings of St. Maximos the Confessor (580–662). Living during the church's flirtation with *monophysitism* (the belief that Jesus had only the divine will), St. Maximos stood firm for *dyothelitism* (the belief that Jesus had two wills, divine and human), a position eventually confirmed by the Sixth Ecumenical Council (680–681).

---

3. *Merriam-Webster.com Dictionary*, "Mystery," https://www.merriam-webster.com/dictionary/mystery.

4. For two nuanced introductions to the complexity of mystery, see Louth, *Discerning the Mystery*; and Dart, "Certainty, Uncertainty and Wisdom."

5. Ware, *Orthodox Way*, 15. Emphasis original.

Part 1: The Mystery

At the time, however, St. Maximos' theological position unfortunately led to his banishment and martyrdom. Happily, his letters were saved and copied, allowing him to influence the direction of Orthodox spirituality.

At the core of his theology is the mystery of the incarnation. It was this event, which God would have accomplished even if Adam and Eve had stayed in the garden, that set the stage for everything else. Even though it was the pinnacle of creation, the incarnation is still something the human mind and intellect can never truly understand. As St. Maximos so eloquently states, "the great mystery of the incarnation remains a mystery eternally. Not only is what is not yet seen of it greater than what has been revealed—for it is revealed merely to the extent that those saved by it can grasp it—but also even what is revealed still remains entirely hidden and is by no means known as it really is."[6]

Buried within this statement about the incarnation is a different way of thinking about the Creator and the world around us. Following the lead of Dionysius the Areopagite (sixth century), St. Maximos draws attention to both the *kataphatic* and *apophatic* approaches to theology. The former approach (*kataphatic* or *cataphatic*) focuses on concepts or values that can be affirmed of God from nature or Scripture. The latter view (*apophatic*) approaches theology from the opposite direction, using negative statements to highlight what God is *not* like rather affirming who he *is*. Hence *apophatic* theology keeps us from misspeaking about God and relying too much on our own intellect as the Creator transcends all that we may think or feel about him. In comparing the two approaches, St. Maximos states:

> If you theologize in an affirmative or *cataphatic* manner, starting from positive statements about God, you make the Logos flesh, for you have no other means of knowing God as cause except from what is visible and tangible. If you theologize in a negative or *apophatic* manner, through the stripping away of positive attributes, you make the Logos spirit or God as He was in His principal

6. Maximos, *Various Texts*, 167.

state with God: starting from absolutely none of the things that can be known, you come in an admirable way to know Him who transcends unknowing.[7]

It is because of these two approaches to theology that St. Maximos can declare that what the incarnation did not reveal is greater than what it did reveal. Rather than trying to unravel the mystery of the incarnation, St. Maximos encourages us to "contemplate with faith the mystery of the divine incarnation and in all simplicity let us simply praise Him who in His great generosity became man for us."[8]

In contrast to this embracement of the mystery, Western European theological studies since the seventeenth century have sought to define and understand all aspects of the faith.[9] This shift in mindset, commonly called the Enlightenment,[10] placed an emphasis on reason and logic to understand the world along with a skepticism towards the ways of the past.[11] The tension of the mystery was broken as the church and culture at large embraced a *kataphatic* approach to life while delegating the *apophatic* approach to the basement of

---

7. Maximos, *Two Hundred Texts*, 147.
8. Maximos, *Various Texts*, 167.
9. Erickson, *Introducing Christian Doctrine*, 32–34.
10. The Enlightenment is a general term used to describe a European cultural and intellectual movement within the seventeenth and eighteenth centuries. Though the Age of Enlightenment has officially ended, the shadow of the movement can still be seen on the shores of North America. Within the movement itself, there were at least three major wings: rationalism, humanism, and romanticism. Of these three wings, my primary concern is with the attachment to certitude embedded in the right or rationalist wing and the philosophical foundationalism that grew out of this attachment. Driven by a desire to remove the uncertainty that naturally arises from humanity's inconsistencies, most Enlightenment thinkers readily adopted some type of foundation upon which they developed their epistemological outlook of life. Though the humanist and romantic wings would critique it, the philosophical foundationalism of the rationalist wing would eventually, as Stanley Grenz and John Franke note, "reformulated thinking in every area of Western society, including theology and religious belief" (Grenz and Franke, *Beyond Foundationalism*, 32). Hence the long shadow cast by the Enlightenment across spatiotemporal space.
11. Olson, *Story of Christian Theology*, 522.

life, to be forgotten in the dusty tomes of history. Those who did try to retain the mystical approach to life were pushed to the edges of Christianity and considered eccentrics or freaks.

The result of this paradigm shift is that the church today has inherited, as noted by American author and pastoral ministry professor Dr. Charles Conniry Jr., "two primary approaches to Christian spirituality: *the way of knowledge* and its reactionary counterpart, *the way of piety*."[12] The former focuses on what we *know* while the latter focuses on what we *do* or *do not do*.[13] Though they appear different on the surface, both approaches are in effect the same in that they "construe the essence of faith in very black-and-white terms—either as the accumulation of knowledge or the acquisition of virtue."[14]

As with most things in life, neither path is mutually exclusive, with individuals and church groups embracing aspects of both the way of knowledge and the way of piety. At the risk of being overly stereotypical, it could be said that those who focus on the way of knowledge tend to place an emphasis on the transmission of information, doctrinal statements, and an intellectual understanding of the Scriptures and theology.[15] The way of piety arose as a reaction to the way of knowledge with adherents emphasizing personal holiness and service towards others.[16] Within North America, the focus on piety led some to embrace a mindset of anti-intellectualism, individualism, and emotionalism.[17]

In contrast to this *kataphatic* approach to life, the way of mystery beckons us towards a third path in which we embrace the tensions of piety and knowledge, knowing and not knowing. The end result of this path is one of love and union with God as St. Maximos notes in his writings:

---

12. Conniry, "Western World's Loss," 28. Emphasis original.
13. Conniry, "Western World's Loss," 32.
14. Conniry, "Western World's Loss," 28.
15. Conniry, "Western World's Loss," 29–30.
16. Conniry, "Western World's Loss," 30–31.
17. Olson, *Story of Christian Theology*, 491.

> When the intellect practices the virtues [i.e., the way of piety] correctly, it advances in moral understanding. When it practices contemplation [i.e., the way of knowledge], it advances in spiritual knowledge. The first leads the spiritual contestant to discriminate between virtue and vice; the second leads the participant to the inner qualities of incorporeal and corporeal things. Finally, the intellect is granted the grace of theology when, *carried on wings of love* beyond these two former stages, it is *taken up into God* and with the help of the Holy Spirit discern [i.e., knowing]—as far as this is possible for the human intellect [i.e., not knowing]—the qualities of God.[18]

At its core, the way of the mystery is, as Dr. Charles Conniry Jr. reminds us, "a way of being in relationship with God, humanity, and creation."[19] It is about the incarnation in which the Creator King became human so that we might know he who is unknowable (e.g., Colossians 1:15–16; John 1:18; 2 Corinthians 4:4–6). "Christ," St. Maximos declares, "is the great hidden mystery, the blessed goal, the purpose for which everything was created."[20]

The Darkness of Unknowing

In the third month after being delivered from slavery in Egypt, the ancient Israelites entered the desert of Sinai and camped before the holy mountain of the Creator (Exodus 19). Following the instructions of Moses, the people sanctified themselves in preparation for the coming of the Creator. On the morning of the third day the mountain shook violently as a dense cloud of smoke covered it. The Lord descended "on it in fire" with the smoke rising upwards "like the smoke of a great furnace" (Exodus 19:18, NET). Though the people were scared, Moses followed the voice of God and "drew near the thick darkness where God was" (Exodus 20:21, NET).

---

18. Maximos, *Four Hundred Texts*, 9. Emphasis added.
19. Conniry, "Western World's Loss," 43.
20. Maximos, *Questions to Thalassius*, quoted in Clément, *Roots of Christian Mysticism*, 39.

Part 1: The Mystery

In pondering this event, St. Maximos saw the darkness into which Moses walked as the "formless and immaterial realm of spiritual knowledge."[21] This, according to St. Maximos, stands in contrast to the tent of meeting that Moses pitched outside the camp for anyone to use who wanted to inquire of the Lord (Exodus 33:7). The tent of meeting was the place where Moses "begins to worship God" while it is in the darkness that he "celebrates the most sacred rites."[22] It is out of the darkness of the mountain top, in which his senses were rendered useless, that Moses truly met the One whom he loved. So much so that his face shined bright with the glow of the light of the Creator long after he left the mountain top (Exodus 34:29–35).

Years later the Spanish Roman Catholic reformer St. John of the Cross (1542–1591) would pen a moving poem called "Dark Night of the Soul" while imprisoned by religious authorities who disagreed with his teachings. Drawing inspiration from the same passage about Moses along with Psalm 18:11 ("He shrouded himself in darkness," NET), St. John describes the journey of a soul who leaves the light of the known to go "into the darkness of the night"[23] in search of its Beloved (i.e., Jesus).[24] Darkness in this sense is not the absence of the Creator but the place where we experience the real tangible presence of God, albeit in a hidden manner similar to how Moses met the Father within the darkness on Mt. Sinai.[25]

Popular culture, however, has twisted the words of St. John's poem about the dark night to mean a time of hardship and pain. That is not what St. John meant. Pain and hardship are part of the human experience while we await the glorious day of the second coming of our Lord. Rather than being about hardships, the dark night of the soul is where we embrace the mystery of the unknown

---

21. Maximos, *Two Hundred Texts*, 133.
22. Maximos, *Two Hundred Texts*, 133.
23. John of the Cross, *Dark Night*, 3.
24. Blin-Bolt, "Darkness as a Metaphor," 19.
25. Blin-Bolt, "Darkness as a Metaphor," 64.

and follow promptings of the Holy Spirit to search for our Beloved.[26] It is a time when we allow the Creator King to purify our hearts and change our lives. Though we might not know what comes next, we walk boldly into the darkness knowing that Jesus awaits us. As Dionysius the Areopagite wrote in his famous work *The Mystical Theology*, "Unto this Darkness which is beyond Light we pray that we may come and may attain unto vision through the loss of sight and knowledge, and that in ceasing thus to see or to know we may learn to know that which is beyond all perception and understanding."[27]

The path of following Jesus is like St. John's poem. In bowing our knees to Jesus, we have to give up what we know to embrace what we do not know. This is true at the very beginning of our journey when we first meet Jesus and it is just as true later on in our walk with him. Similar to how Abraham had to embark on a journey into an unknown land at the instructions of the Lord before he learned his fate (Genesis 12:1–7) or how Moses had to walk into the darkness of the cloud before he met the Lord (Exodus 20:21), we must leave behind what we know and journey into the mysteries of the unknown, where the Creator awaits.[28] In describing this journey, Bishop Kallistos Ware comments:

> We go out from the known to the unknown, we advance from light into darkness. We do not simply proceed from the darkness of ignorance into the light of knowledge, but we go forward from the light of partial knowledge into a greater knowledge which is so much more profound that it can only be described as the "darkness of unknowing."[29]

Though all of this may sound strange to those who embrace a purely *kataphatic* approach to life, Marie-Dominique Blin-Bolt rightly notes that "metaphors of inwardness, ascent, light and darkness are central to Christianity and are a feature of *apophatic*

---

26. Blin-Bolt, "Darkness as a Metaphor," 63–64; Margaret Kim Peterson, "Introduction," in John of the Cross, *Dark Night*, xv–xvi; Sittser, *Water from a Deep Well*, 184–85.

27. *Mystical Theology*, in Dionysius, *Dionysius the Areopagite*, 100–101.

28. Ware, *Orthodox Way*, 13.

29. Ware, *Orthodox Way*, 13–14.

theology."[30] They are the words of mystery in which we finite creatures try to describe the One who is beyond our understanding. In embracing the way of mystery and the tension of *kataphatic/apophatic* theology, the hope is that we might come into union with the Creator King, who loved us so much that he left the glories of heaven to walk with us within the bounds of time and physicality.

> **"Dark Night of the Soul" by St. John of the Cross**[31]
> Into the darkness of the night
> With heart ache kindled into love,
> Oh blessed chance!
> I stole me forth unseen,
> My house being wrapped in sleep.
>
> Into the darkness, and yet safe
> By secret stair and in disguise,
> Oh gladsome hap!
> In darkness, and in secret I crept forth,
> My house being wrapt in sleep.
>
> Into the happy night
> In secret, seen of none,
> Nor saw I ought,
> Without, or other light or guide,
> Save that which in my heart did burn.
>
> This fire it was that guided me
> More certainly than midday sun,
> Where he did wait,
> He that I knew imprinted on my heart,
> In place, where none appeared.
>
> Oh Night, that led me, guiding night,
> Oh Night far sweeter than the Dawn;
> Oh Night, that did so then unite
> The Loved with His Beloved,
> Transforming Lover in Beloved.

---

30. Blin-Bolt, "Darkness as a Metaphor," 33.
31. John of the Cross, *Dark Night*, 3–4.

Loving the Unknowable

On my blossoming breast,
Alone for him entire was kept,
He fell asleep,
Whilst I caressed,
And fanned him with the cedar fan.

The breeze from forth the battlements,
As then it tossed his hair about,
With his fair hand
He touched me lightly on the neck,
And reft me of my senses in a swoon.

I lay quite still, all mem'ry lost,
I leaned my face upon my Loved One's breast;
I knew no more, in sweet abandonment
I cast away my care,
And left it all forgot amdist the lilies fair.

— 3 —

Through the Darkness

When a train goes through a tunnel and it gets dark, you don't throw away the ticket and jump off. You sit still and trust the engineer.

—CORRIE TEN BOOM[1]

People like Keith have trained themselves over many years to seek the counsel of friends, even when they are tempted to isolate themselves. To trust in the faith of others, even when they doubt their own beliefs. To worship and read God's Word, even when they don't feel like it.

—PETE GREIG[2]

THERE IS SOMETHING ABOUT a rainstorm that cries out to be watched. Most of the time, it is a quiet cry that is easily dismissed. Yet there are those occasional rainstorms that yell at the top of their lungs for all to come and watch. This was neither that type of storm nor the other. Rather it was one of darkness.

---

1. Ten Boom, *Jesus Is Victor*, 183.
2. Greig, *Dirty Glory*, 36.

Through the Darkness

There were four of us that night, all teenagers thrilled to be camping on our grandparents' farm without parental supervision. In our zeal to distance ourselves from the trappings of modern conveniences, we chose to pitch our tents on the back side of the twenty-acre farm in the foothills of the Ozark Mountains within the Cherokee Nation. At first everything seemed fine as night fell and we bedded down inside our tent. Our excitement quickly fled as a rainstorm broke over us that night, bring with it not only rain, but pain as my brother's lungs betrayed him, seeking to suffocate him rather than giving him life. He was having an asthma attack, and though he had been hospitalized for such attacks before, we delayed the wet trip through the darkness in a vain attempt to retain the youthful thrill of surviving without our parents.

Finally, the time came when I could no longer stand by watching him struggle for every breath. Grabbing his arm, I helped him out of the tent and into the rainy darkness of the storm. Ever so slowly I started forward with him leaning on my shoulder, confident of my ability to successfully navigate the night trip through the woods. Yet as the minutes ticked by, a sense of dread creeped over me as I realized that we were lost. The trees glared at me through the lightning flashes, daring me to walk under their branches while the landmarks I knew should be there were not to be found. Step by step, gasp by gasp, we walked forward into the darkness not knowing where we were going.

Joining an Ongoing Story

Alice was another lost soul wandering through a strange land trying to find her way back home. Along the way she stumbled upon a cat sitting on a tree branch. Initially frighten, she overcame her fear and asked the cat which way she ought to go. The cat, being a bit mad, responded with perhaps the most powerful statement ever recorded: "That depends a good deal on where you want to get to."[3] This advice, while originally given in the context of spatial

---

3. Carroll, *Alice's Adventures*, 75.

dimensions, is equally valid in a temporal and spiritual sense. If we, the followers of Jesus, really want to find our Beloved in the darkness of the unknown, we need to first know where we are going. It may sound strange to think about knowing where you are going while embracing the mystery of the unknown. Yet, it is exactly in this paradox that we find the truth of life.

Years ago, when the people of Israel were on the edge of the unknown with Jerusalem and the temple about to be destroyed, the Creator sent the prophet Jeremiah to tell them not to worry. Rather they were to "stand at the crossroads" between the known and unknown and "ask for the ancient paths" (Jeremiah 6:16, NIV). It would be in walking down the ancient paths of those who followed the call of the Creator King that they would find rest for their souls.

The same is true for us today. We are the heirs of an ancient faith with roots back to the very beginning of time. We are not the first people to start this journey, nor will we be the last. Accordingly, we can look backwards to those who have gone ahead of us to find our way forward. As author of Hebrews reminds us, we are "surrounded by . . . a great cloud of witnesses" (Hebrews 12:1, NIV) who are cheering us on, encouraging us to finish the race set before us.

Philadelphia Archbishop Charles Chaput of the Roman Catholic Church once remarked that "Americans have never liked history . . . [for] the past comes with obligations on the present, and the most cherished illusion of American life is that we can remake ourselves at will."[4] This self-imposed historical amnesia causes us to have an unhealthy "egocentric obsession with the present"[5] as noted by Brian Zahnd. Once we embrace the concept that we are part of an ongoing story that is bigger than ourselves, then everything changes. No longer is the Christian faith about me or what I can get out of it. No longer is it just about our particular group within Christianity or our nation. Rather our eyes are

---

4. Chaput, "Remembering Who We Are."
5. Zahnd, *Water to Wine*, 1349.

opened to the bigger picture of God's rule and reign, which spans both time and space.

Walking with Jesus

When the prophet Jeremiah first told the people of God to walk in the ancient path, he was referring to the stories of Noah, Abraham, Joseph, Moses, Deborah, David, Elijah, and others. These were the heroes of the faith to whom the people were to look back toward and learn how to find peace for their hearts. What is interesting is that a lot of these folks didn't have the Scriptures to look at and read. And even those who had the Scriptures only had a portion of them as they were still being written. I emphasize this historical fact as a lot of us assume that the written Word is the only way to know God. A look through the Scriptures themselves, not to mention history, tells us that while they are important, the Creator King is much, much bigger than the Bible.

The heroes of the faith God told his people to emulate had a personal encounter with the Living God, who called them forth on a journey into the unknown. Noah, for example, heard the Lord calling him to build an ark in preparation for rainstorm in a land where it had never rained (Genesis 6:9—7:24). I'm sure everyone around him, including his wife and children, thought he was crazy. Yet he bravely embraced the mystery of the unknown and trusted the voice of the Lord.

Joseph the son of Jacob was another hero who stayed faithful through hardship and pain. He had a dream that he thought was from God, so he told his family. Instead of rejoicing in the fact that God was speaking to him, they got mad at him. After the second dream, they beat him up and sold him to a slave trader (Genesis 37:12–36). If anyone had reason to distrust the Lord, it would be Joseph. Think about it: What would you do if you woke up in the middle of the night after a dream? Would you base your entire life on that that dream? Or would you dismiss it as a fluke? What about if your family betrayed you because of that dream? If it was me, I would have gotten mad at God and told him to leave me alone.

Part 1: The Mystery

Joseph, however, continued to walk after the Creator King despite his circumstances just like his great-grandfather, Abraham.

Similar stories could be told of each of the other heroes of the faith who walked the ancient path. Each of them had an encounter with the Living God that changed their life. Each day of each year that followed that encounter, they walked forward into the darkness trusting God to guide them. Not only did they trust the King with their spirit, they trusted him with their earthly existence as well as the lives of their family members. A quick scan through the Old Testament reveals a number of women and men of God who left behind all they knew in order to obey the words given to them by the Creator.

I guess you could say that before we can really answer the Cheshire Cat's question of where we are going, we have to answer the question of whom we are traveling with. To walk in the ancient paths of the heroes of old is to walk beside the Living Creator. Amazingly enough the Living God clothed himself in flesh and walked this earth as a man to show us the way forward into the darkness of the unknown. "For He [Jesus]," St. Maximos wrote, "has passed through all things for us by the dispensation of His incarnation, so that we, by following Him, may pass through all that is sequent to Him and so come to be with Him."[6] The ministry, death, resurrection, and ascension of Jesus ushered in the new age of God's kingdom in a way the heroes could only dream about. As the writer of the book of Hebrews reminds us, they only looked forward to the promise of what we walk in daily (Hebrews 11:39–40).

Jesus is our companion into and through the darkness of the unknown of this journey of life. It is he who beckons us to leave behind what we know and embrace the mystery of uncertainty. It could be the mystery of moving to another geographical location like Abraham, Moses, or the people of Israel who heard the voice of Jeremiah. Or it could be the mystery of embracing new concepts and ideas, like the apostle Paul and others of his day. No matter what type of mystery it is, Jesus walks before us, with us, and after us. For Jesus, St. Maximos says in an echo of St. John the

6. Maximos, *Two Hundred Texts*, 142.

Apostle, "is the way, the door, the key and the kingdom. He is the way because He guides; He is the key because He both opens and is opened to those found worthy to receive divine blessings; He is the door because He gives admittance; He is the kingdom because He is inherited and because He enters by participation into all things."[7] With Jesus as a guide, we know that all will be well even if it means walking through the valley of the shadow of death.

Following Those before Us

As I stumbled through the woods that rainy night, my eyes eagerly scanned the forest around me at each flash of lightning. When I had first started off with my brother, I was following an old dirt road that cut through my grandparents' farm and led to the house. Somewhere along the line I had drifted off this road and into the surrounding woods, losing all sense of direction in the process. Yet I knew that if I could just find a recognizable landmark I would be able to find that road again and get help for my brother.

Then out of the darkness stood a fence post. It wasn't anything special, just a normal everyday t-post like the ones before it and the ones after it. Yet at that moment that t-post, and the barbed-wire fence connected to it, was the most beautiful thing on the planet. Though it may sound strange, that fence told me that someone else had been there before me and that they had forged a path through the woods. The only problem was that I didn't know if I should follow the fence to the left or to the right. Or if I would be better off trying to find another more recognizable landmark.

Our journey through the darkness of life is a lot like my blundering trip through the woods that night. The circumstances of life will sometimes force us to strike out into the unknown though we may want to stay where we are. We may even start off walking on a familiar path only to find ourselves lost in confusion far from any recognizable landmarks. At some point during these times of wandering we will most likely stumble across some type of marker left

---

7. Maximos, *Two Hundred Texts*, 154.

Part 1: The Mystery

behind by those who went before us, just like I bumped into that fence post that night. And when we do stumble upon a marker, it can be hard to know which direction to go.

Luckily for us, some of the people before us kept a record of what they did and what the Lord did around and through them. We call this record the Bible and it was written over approximately 1,500 years by at least forty different authors. Within its pages we find life and encouragement to keep walking into the darkness of the unknown. In his *Ascetic Discourse*, the fifth-century abbot St. Neilos the Ascetic encourages the brethren around him to "recall the lives of the men of old, written by the Holy Spirit: here appropriate examples can be found to bring each man to the truth, whatever his way of life."[8] By following St. Neilos's advice and in reading the Scriptures, we can hear about a farmer named Gideon who nervously stepped out in faith and followed the Lord's command. Or we can hear how a few fishermen and a tax collector changed the course of human history. Furthermore, when we are awakened in the night by a thought-provoking dream, we can open up the Scriptures and read about Joseph and his dreams. In reading these stories, we can build up our faith and courage as we see how God worked in and through average folks just like us.

In addition to reading the ancient stories, we can also talk to those around us. Years ago, when I was in my late twenties, I found myself lost in the darkness of life surrounded by lots of new concepts about God and life. As I pondered these things, I realized that I needed some help before I could fully embrace them. Looking around me, I asked some women and men in my church whom I perceived were further along the ancient path to join me for coffee. Gathering together, we allowed ourselves to be completely honest with each other and ourselves. No concept or issue was off the table as we all wanted to fully vet the new concepts we were learning. If the ideas were not in line with the person of Jesus and the Scriptures, then we didn't want to walk down that path. This monthly "Kingdom Coffee" group soon became a guide for us as we traveled through the darkness of life.

---

8. Neilos, *Ascetic Discourse*, 228.

In thinking about the importance of having companions and instructors along the journey, St. Neilos comments:

> To master any art requires time and much instruction; can the art of arts alone be mastered without being learnt? No one without experience would go in for farming; nor would someone who has never been taught medicine try to practice as a doctor. The first would be condemned for making good farmland barren and weed-infested; the second, for making the sick worse instead of better. The only art which the uninstructed dare to practice, because they think it the simplest of all, is that of the spiritual way. What is difficult the majority regard as easy; and what Paul says he has not yet apprehended (cf. Phil. 3:12), they claim to know through and through, although they do not know even this: that they are totally ignorant.[9]

Though these words were written in the context of a monastery, their message remains equally important for those of us outside the monastery walls. We all need teachers and companions who can advise and counsel us as we walk along the spiritual way. Sadly, it is easy for those of us in the United States of America to forget about the value of instruction and community. We are surrounded by an individualist society with a high value being placed on the views of the individual. And while there is some good that comes out of such a society, we must also recognize the value of belonging to a faith that is bigger and older than any of us. "We do not read the Bible as isolated individuals," Bishop Kallistos Ware of the Eastern Orthodox Church reminds us, "interpreting it solely by the light of our private understanding, or in terms of current theories about source, form or redaction criticism. We read it as members of the Church, in communion with all the other members throughout the ages."[10]

Theology, after all, is an ongoing conversation among those who have encountered the Creator through Jesus the Christ.[11] And

---

9. Neilos, *Ascetic Discourse*, 215.
10. Ware, *Orthodox Way*, 110.
11. Grenz and Franke, *Beyond Foundationalism*, 233.

in thinking about the community of believers, we must not limit ourselves to only those who are currently alive. Christianity, we must always remember, does not belong solely to the living but also to those who have confessed Christ throughout the ages. Accordingly, there is wisdom in listening to and learning from both those who have walked before us in history as well as those living around us at this moment. It is a both-and concept in which we seek the counsel of others even when we are tempted to isolate ourselves.

Guided by the Spirit

Do you remember that fence I stumbled upon in middle of night while lost with my brother? Knowing that I had to keep moving, I randomly picked a direction and started to follow the fence, which led me to a corner post that marked the edge of my grandparents' property. As we approached the fence corner, memories of helping my father install that post came flooding over me. Working together, we had dug a deep hole to set a strong center post before bending over and securing two other posts to the main one. It was a type of trinity; three posts connected together to create a corner post that could withstand the pressure placed on it by the fence wires. (This post, by the way, was the landmark I needed to find my way back home and get help for my brother, who survived that crazy circuitous trip through the woods.)

The Holy Spirit is the corner post for us as we journey into the mysterious darkness of the unknown. As part of the Godhead, he is securely anchored to the Father and the Son. No amount of pressure or force can move him, giving us peace and hope as we know that he loves and cares for us. Though the world around us may fall into chaos, to find the corner post of the Holy Spirit is to know that we will be alright. Death and sorrow may come, but we walk through the valley of the shadow of death with our Lord and Guide.

Years ago, on that fateful evening before he was betrayed, Jesus looked at his disciples and had compassion on them. He knew that within a few hours their entire lives would be forever changed.

They would be scared and confused as all that they had ever known would be taken away. In comforting them, Jesus told them about the Holy Spirit, who would come and guide them through the darkness (John 15:26—16:15). It is interesting to me that Jesus did not tell the disciples to read the Hebrew Scriptures (i.e., the Old Testament) or to take a vote to determine their future. While community and the Bible are great—as previously mentioned—they do not hold everything together. That role belongs to the Holy Spirit for it is the Spirit who, according to St. Maximos, "leads those who seek the spiritual principles and qualities of salvation to an understanding of them."[12]

The Scriptures, for example, may be destroyed or banned from our specific geographical location. Or we may find ourselves, like a lot of our sisters and brothers throughout history, unable to read them through a lack of training or because they have never been translated into our language. Either way, we can still find our way through the darkness by holding on to the Holy Spirit and walking with our Beloved. The same is true if for some reason we find ourselves alone with no other Jesus followers around us. Or, perhaps, the community to which we belong is going a direction that doesn't seem to flow from the heart of the Creator. In those cases, we can rest assured that Jesus is with us and Spirit of the Living God will guide us through the darkness.

We don't normally think about it, but Abraham, Joseph, Moses, David, and the rest all braved this cruel world without having the Spirit living within them. Having the Spirit of the Living God living inside us is amazing (e.g., Acts 2:32–33; 2 Corinthians 1:22; Ephesians 1:13–14)! Though we may take it for granted, it is a fairly new development in the course of human history. The ancient heroes of the Old Testament sometimes had to go for days, weeks, years, and perhaps even decades between encounters with the Living God. We can learn a lot about tenacity and staying the course from these ancient heroes.

In returning to our conversation partner St. Maximos, the following paragraphs from his book *Two Hundred Texts on Theology*

---

12. Maximos, *Various Texts*, 240.

and the Incarnate Dispensation of the Son of God summarize what it means to walk into the darkness of the unknown with our Beloved, Jesus of Nazareth:

> Before His visible advent in the flesh the Logos of God dwelt among the patriarchs and prophets in a spiritual manner, prefiguring the mysteries of His advent. After His incarnation He is present in a similar way not only to those who are still beginners, nourishing them spiritually and leading them towards the maturity of divine perfection, but also to the perfect, secretly pre-delineating in them the features of His future advent as if in an ikon.
>
> Just as the teachings of the Law and the prophets, being harbingers of the coming advent of the Logos in the flesh, guide our souls to Christ (cf. Gal. 3:24), so the glorified incarnate Logos of God is Himself a harbinger of His spiritual advent, leading our souls forward by His own teachings to receive His divine and manifest advent. He does this ceaselessly, by means of the virtues converting those found worthy from the flesh to the spirit. And He will do it at the end of the age, making manifest what has hitherto been hidden from all men.[13]

Though the darkness of the unknown is scary—whether it be the darkness of new ideas/concepts or the unknown of the future—we know we do not have to walk through the darkness alone. We can bravely set out into the unknown with our eyes set firmly on our destination with Jesus walking beside us, while following the markers left behind by those who have gone on before us as recorded in the Scriptures and throughout history by the wider community of believers. And through it all, we are guided by the Holy Spirit, who dwells within us. Together we will cross the sea of chaos and climb Mount Zion to worship in the temple of the Most High.

---

13. Maximos, *Two Hundred Texts*, 144.

— 4 —

Beyond Knowing

> Nature . . . provides ample evidence that there is a lot more to God than meets the eye. Being mindful of our surroundings is all it takes for us to appreciate the fact that the One who made our world delights in paradox and mystery. In the light of our surroundings, it makes little sense to assume that we have the capacity to comprehend truth in its fullness—and to be absolutely certain about that fact.
>
> —DR. CHARLES CONNIRY JR.[1]

THERE ARE THREE LITTLE life-giving words that are rarely uttered in the halls of certainty: "I don't know." We all want to be known as the person who knows everything, rather than being known as someone who doesn't know a thing. It is true that the phrase "I don't know" is uttered more in Western culture than in the East. Those of us who grew up under the shadow of the Enlightenment tend to have an easier time confessing our ignorance. However, I would say that it is a false sense of ignorance as our "enlightened" culture uses the lack of knowledge as an excuse to search for more. For us "I don't know" really means, "Let me learn more and then I will tell you the answer."

---

1. Conniry, "Western World's Loss," 28.

Part 1: The Mystery

In the *Verba Seniorum*, the *Sayings of the Fathers*, there is a story about Abbot Antony that highlights the freedom of not knowing. Written during the third or fourth century CE, the story tells of a time when some old men came to see Abbot Antony. Wishing to prove them, Antony brought the conversation around to the Scriptures. Starting with the youngest, he asked them about this or that verse. Each one answered the best they could, but to each Antony told them that they had not yet found the answer. Finally, he came to the Abbot Joseph, who simply answered, "I know not." At this response, Abbot Antony exclaimed, "Verily the Abbot Joseph alone hath found the road, who saith that he doth not know."[2]

To find the road of the mystery is to recognize that we brave souls who journey into the darkness of the unknown in search of our Beloved are seeing only a reflection of what is truly real (1 Corinthians 13:12). And as with all reflections, how much we see and understand is dependent upon the mirror into which we stare. Hence to declare "I don't know" is a mark of humility for none of us truly know or understand the darkness through which we walk.

No Simple Answers

There is a myth that is so pervasive and widespread that most of us believe its lies without thinking. What, you may ask, is this myth? It is the myth of common sense. Or, to use different words, it is the belief that people everywhere have the ability, wisdom, and understanding to come to the same conclusion as we would or do the same thing that we would do in a given situation. After all, some things are just plain common sense. Or so the argument goes.

The problem with this chain of thought is that everyone on the planet has a different way of seeing the world. We are all unique beings with our own experiences, abilities, thoughts, and actions. Taken together, it means that there is no such thing as "common sense" as we all have our own sense of the world around us.

---

2. Waddell, ed., *Desert Fathers*, 121.

Beyond Knowing

True, as some might say, there are some shared cultural events, precepts, and beliefs. After all, societies work specifically because of shared cultural norms (i.e., attitudes and behaviors that are considered normal with a culture, such as how one is to greet each other). However, I would argue that just because we might agree on broad cultural norms, this doesn't necessarily equate to having a common sense that is shared among humanity. The world is too large and too multifaceted for such a phenomenon.

I highlight this myth because it shows how strongly the desire is within us for simple answers. We want a simple world with simple answers to simple questions. We desperately desire a world that is easy to understand and easy to move around in with folks who see things the same way as we do. Reality, however, isn't so simple or nice. As the English writer and lay theologian C. S. Lewis once remarked, "Besides being complicated, reality, in my experience, is usually odd. It is not neat, not obvious, not what you expect . . . Reality, in fact, is usually something you could not have guessed."[3]

So, what should we do? If reality really is complex and strange, as it seems to be, then how do we approach things? How do we move forward through the darkness of the unknown while surrounded by paradoxes and oddities? To quote C. S. Lewis once again, the answer is to "leave behind all these boys' philosophies—these over-simple answers. The problem is not simple, and the answer is not going to be simpler either."[4]

Accordingly let us stop trying to reduce the complexity of this world into simple answers. Let us be honest with ourselves and others and acknowledge the complexity of the world in which we live. And in doing so let us also recognize the complexity and mysterious wonder of the Creator. He is not a simple being who can be described in simple terms or made to dance to the tune of our thoughts and desires. The focus of Christianity, Bishop Kallistos Ware reminds us, is not to "provide easy answers to every question,

---

3. Lewis, *Mere Christianity*, 48.
4. Lewis, *Mere Christianity*, 48.

but to make us progressively aware of a mystery. God is not so much the object of our knowledge as the cause of our wonder."[5]

God is God. He is beyond our thinking and understanding (e.g., Ecclesiastes 11:5; Isaiah 55:8–9; Psalm 145:3; 1 Corinthians 2:11). Try as we might, our words and simple descriptions of him will always fall short of fully capturing the wonder of who he really is. St. Gregory of Nyssa, a fourth-century church father, put it this way: "Anyone who tries to describe the ineffable Light in language is truly a liar—not because he hates the truth, but because of the inadequacy of his description."[6]

Never Stop Searching

If there are no simple answers and God is beyond all that we can ever conceive, should we then give up searching and resign ourselves to a life of ignorance? Ignorance, it is said, is bliss. St. Maximos, in embracing the mystery of knowing and not knowing, encourages us to continue to search as "the person who loves God values knowledge of God more than anything created by God and pursues such knowledge ardently and ceaselessly."[7] The Scriptures themselves echo this advice with encouragement for those of us who willing bravely venture into the darkness of the unknown after our Beloved (e.g., Proverbs 8:17; Deuteronomy 4:29; Jeremiah 29:13; Matthew 22:37; Acts 17:27; Hebrews 11:6). It is as the Irish postmodern philosopher Peter Rollins once said: "that which we cannot speak of is the one thing about whom and to whom we must never stop speaking."[8]

Jesus, true God of true God, who was sent by the Father to reveal himself to humanity (Hebrews 1:2), told his followers, among whom we are numbered, to actively ask, seek, and knock on the door of the unknown (Matthew 7:7–8; Luke 11:9–10). It is the

---

5. Ware, *Orthodox Way*, 14.
6. Gregory of Nyssa, *On Virginity*, quoted in Ware, *Orthodox Way*, 24.
7. Maximos, *Four Hundred Texts*, 53.
8. Rollins, *How (Not) to Speak*, xiv.

asking, the seeking, and the knocking that is important rather than the receiving, the finding, and the opening.⁹ We are to continually seeking after the Lord, knocking on the closed doors of life and asking for the "good gifts" of the Father (Matthew 7:9–11, NET). The Father, for his part, has promised to infuse us with his Spirit who will guide us into the unknown while revealing the mysteries of his wisdom to us along the way (e.g., Luke 11:13; John 16:13; 1 Corinthians 2:6–16). "The Lord," St. Mark the Ascetic (fifth century) wrote, "is hidden in His own commandments, and He is to be found there in the measure that He is sought."¹⁰

Even here we are faced with a paradox as we are not to focus on the gifts of the Father or the revealed mysteries of the Spirit. Jesus is to be the sole focus of our desire. It is Jesus whom we seek as we walk into the darkness of the unknown even as it is him who walks with us. "A true seeking after God," Peter Rollins reminds us, "results from an experience of God which one falls in love with for no reason other than finding God irresistibly lovable. In this way the lovers of God are the ones who are the most passionately in search of God."¹¹ We are, to quote the apostle Paul, to know nothing "except Jesus Christ, and him crucified" (1 Corinthians 2:2, NET).

Being Open Handed with Our Faith

Human nature is a strange thing when you really stop and think about it. We will resist changing with everything within us; yet when we do change, we forget the struggle and wonder why everyone else hasn't changed. Going into the darkness of the unknown is a scary thing. We should never trivialize it or forget the pain that goes with stepping out beyond our norm. Rather we should remember the journey and have grace for those along the way. As the apostle Paul tells us, we are to clothe ourselves with "compassion,

---

9. Rollins, *How (Not) to Speak*, 53.
10. Mark, "On the Spiritual Law," 123.
11. Rollins, *How (Not) to Speak*, 53.

kindness, humility, gentleness, and patience" (Colossians 3:12, NIV) while helping and forgiving those around us.

Humility is a virtue that doesn't get talked about very often. We will talk about compassion, kindness, gentleness, and, at times, patience. But humility is something else... something different. While the other virtues are directed *outward* toward other people, humility is directed *inward*. It is, however, the "highest of all blessings" in the eyes of St. Maximos, the one that "conserves other blessings and destroys their opposites."[12] Similarly St. Bernard of Clairvaux (1090–1153) defined humility as "the virtue by which a man recognizes his own unworthiness because he really knows himself."[13]

Walking in humility along the path of mystery into the darkness of the unknown means being openhanded with our journey and being willing to admit that we might be wrong. It is putting to death the pride and certainty that comes with having to have everything figured out. To embrace humanity is therefore to always be seeking and learning while never growing conceited about our interpretations of the Scripture lest our "intellect fall victim to blasphemy"[14] as St. Mark the Ascetic warned.

It is a recognition that our understanding of the Scriptures and the work of the Creator in the world remains a matter of personal perspective and interpretation while appreciating the role of the Holy Spirit in guiding us "into all truth" (John 16:13, NET).[15] Though we might study the Scriptures for hours and hours and though we might pursue higher education and read multiple books, at the end we are to hold out our thoughts and concepts about the Almighty with an open hand and a willingness to be wrong. We are to become fools, as St. Paul the Apostle encouraged, rejecting the wisdom of our minds, so that we can become wise with Christ (1 Corinthians 3:18–23).

Being openhanded and humble with our interpretations of the Scriptures also does not mean that we cannot stand strong on

---

12. Confessor, "Various Texts," 282.
13. Bernard, *Bernard of Clairvaux*, 103.
14. Mark, *On the Spiritual Law*, 111.
15. Smith, *Who's Afraid of Post-Modernism?*, 121.

Beyond Knowing

our beliefs. We are not to be "tossed back and forth by the waves and blown here and there by every wind of teaching and by the cunning and craftiness of men in their deceitful scheming" (Ephesians 4:14, NIV). Rather we are to stand strong on the foundation of Jesus, knowing that we are part of a family of believers who have endured throughout the ages (Hebrews 10–11; 1 Peter 5:6–11).

Speaking of family, the Creator God has children all over the globe and within the different streams of Christianity. There are things within the Roman Catholic, Eastern Orthodox, Oriental Orthodox, Pentecostal, Charismatic, Evangelical, Anabaptist, and mainline Protestant streams of Christianity that are wonderful and beautiful. Accordingly, we need to actively communicate with our sisters and brothers from different cultural, ecclesiastical, and philosophical traditions while being open and honest about our own beliefs.[16] It is acceptable to hold on to the doctrines and customs of our tradition as long as we humbly admit that these convictions and beliefs are comfortable to us and may not fit everyone who follows the Creator King.

I know some people look at all the streams and denominations of Christianity and see something broken. I, however, see a multifaceted God working within a complex and crazy world. Each church group represents a part of the fullness of the King, who is at work in that part of the world. None of us fully understand the mysterious wonders of the Creator King, who breathed life into existence. Accordingly, let us love and learn from all the various parts of the church as we all walk openhanded into the darkness of the unknown. May we echo the words of Abbot Joseph, who found the road of the mystery while passionately pursuing Jesus with three little words: "I know not."

---

16. Erickson, *Introducing Christian Doctrine*, 37.

PART 2

The Way

It's not enough to believe in Jesus; we also have to believe in the Jesus way! (For that matter, I'm not quite sure what it means to "believe in Jesus" without believing in the Jesus way.) If we don't believe in the Jesus way, we won't know the things that make for peace.

—BRIAN ZAHND[1]

Paul then went straight to the meeting place. He had the run of the place for three months, doing his best to make the things of the kingdom of God real and convincing to them. But then resistance began to form as some of them began spreading evil rumors through the congregation about the Christian way of life. So Paul left, taking the disciples with him, and set up shop in the school of Tyrannus, holding class there daily. He did this for two years, giving everyone in the province of Asia, Jews as well as Greeks, ample opportunity to hear the Message of the Master.

—ST. LUKE THE EVANGELIST[2]

---

1. Zahnd, *Farewell to Mars*, 141.
2. Acts 19:8–10, MSG.

— 5 —

Allegiance to the King

You will not find a greater help than Jesus in all your life . . . Let your soul, then, trust in Christ, let it call on Him and never fear; for it fights, not alone, but with the aid of a mighty King, Jesus Christ, Creator of all that is, both bodiless and embodied, visible and invisible.

—ST. HESYCHIOS THE PRIEST[1]

EVERY MORNING AT 8:30 a.m. during the school year my son lines up with his classmates to recite three pledges before starting the day. They start by reciting the Pledge of Allegiance to the Flag[2] before moving on to the Pledge to the Christian Flag[3] and the Pledge to the Bible.[4] Though these young students may not realize the

---

1. Hesychios, *On Watchfulness and Holiness*, 169.
2. Pledge of Allegiance to the Flag "I pledge allegiance to the Flag of the United States of America, and to the Republic for which it stands, one Nation under God, indivisible, with liberty and justice for all."
3. Pledge to the Christian Flag: "I pledge allegiance to the Christian Flag and to the Savior for whose Kingdom it stands. One Savior, crucified, risen, and coming again with life and liberty to all who believe."
4. Pledge to the Bible: "I pledge allegiance to the Bible, God's Holy Word, I will make it a lamp unto my feet and a light unto my path and will hide its words in my heart that I might not sin against God."

full impact of their words, they are declaring their loyalty to the nation they live in (i.e., United States of America), their religion (i.e., Christianity), and their holy book (i.e., the Bible).

I would wager a guess that there are millions of people around the world reciting similar pledges. They may even recite these pledges in the same order—giving allegiance first to their nation (e.g., USA, Cherokee, India, China, Israel, Russia, Canada, etc.), then to their religion (e.g., Christianity, Judaism, Islam, Hindu, Wicca, Atheism, etc.), and finally to their holy writings (e.g., Bible, Koran, Tripitaka, Vedas, etc.). I would further guess that most of these people, Jesus followers include, don't even think twice about the pledges they are reciting. After all, it is normal to love the nation you live in, the religion you follow, and the holy writings you read.

Yet, if I may vocalize a nagging question in the back of my head, should a follower of Jesus pledge their loyalty and allegiance to a nation, religion, or holy book? And if so, should we be concerned about the order in which we pledge our allegiance? Say, instead of pledging our loyalty to our nation first, maybe we should pledge our allegiance to our religion, our holy writings, and then to our nation—or should we just stop saying the pledges all together?

Jesus followers throughout history have come to different conclusions concerning those questions. They are not easy questions to answer as they have wide-ranging implications for how we live our lives and how we interact with the world around us. For my part, I go back and forth between saying all three pledges, saying some of them, and not saying them at all. My country, religion, and holy writings have all impacted my life to a degree that words cannot fully express. Yet despite of my love for all three, there's a war deep inside of me for I know how my love for my nation, religion, and holy writings can, and does, compete for my love for Jesus. And that concerns me.

Jesus of Nazareth

I was first introduced to Jesus by my parents, who met him from their parents, who likewise met the King through the influence of their parents. I remember early-morning livestock feedings on the farm with my father talking about the Creator or times under the hood of a vehicle talking about doing all things unto the King. There were also times of talking with my mother about the strange and odd verses in the Scriptures that didn't seem to make sense. Though some might think that this genealogy would lead to a lackluster religion more concerned about keeping tradition than knowing the person of Jesus, that wasn't the case for me. Somehow my parents had managed to escape the religiosity and skepticism of the day, even while feeling the pain and disappointment that often leaks out from the rotting corpses housed in whitewashed tombs. And in doing so they taught me to love Jesus and watch for his presence in all areas of life.

These early lessons of seeing past the trappings of religion to find Jesus helped me navigate what American pastor Ken Wilson calls "the witch's brew of politics, cultural conflict, moralism, and religious meanness that seems so closely connected with those who count themselves the special friends of Jesus."[5] Sadly, throughout history there have always been people who have used Jesus to support their own political and religious agendas. This is especially true for those in power in the United States of America, to the point that to "millions of people around the world, Jesus Christ is synonymous with Western society and America" as noted by Carl Medearis, an international expert in the field of Arab-American and Muslim-Christian relations.[6]

In going back to the Scriptures, we find that the central message of Jesus of Nazareth as recorded in the Scriptures was the coming of the kingdom of God (e.g., Matthew 4:17; 9:35; Mark 1:14b–15; Luke 4:43). This announcement was an end-time or eschatological message declaring that the long-awaited reign of the Creator King had begun. No longer were the people of God waiting for the promised day of the Lord when all would be made right. The rule and reign of the Creator King had come in and through Jesus himself.

5. Wilson, *Jesus Brand Spirituality*, 1.
6. Medearis, *Speaking of Jesus*, 61.

Part 2: The Way

Jesus, however, was not alone when he spoke about the kingdom of God. During the first century, when he walked the earth, there were multiple views of the kingdom of God and how that kingdom was manifested in real life.[7] Jesus could have embraced the way of piety promoted by the Pharisees or that of the Essenes. He also had the option of following the path of the Sadducees, the religious priests and rulers of the day, who found wealth and power through their partnership with the Roman Empire. The Romans themselves would have loved it if Jesus would have endorsed their way of life. After all, they were the greatest nation in the world at the time with an empire that stretched across three continents. Or if Jesus did not like the pagan-worshiping Romans being in the land of promise, he could have joined one of the resistance movements active at the time and fought to take back the land for God. There were plenty of people at the time who would have loved to make Jesus king of Israel (John 6:15). All he needed to do was say the word and the revolution would have begun.

Jesus, however, did not and does not "endorse any other way, any other moral code except his own. Jesus was [and is] exclusively the Way"[8] as Carl Medearis reminds us. Hence, he stood boldly between all these groups and proclaimed the way of mystery in declaring that the kingdom of God:

- is here (e.g., Matthew 3:2; 4:17; 12:28; Luke 16:16–17; 17:20–21)
- is in the future (e.g., Matthew 5:3; 21:28–45; Luke 22:29–30)
- is coming soon (e.g., Mark 1:15; 9:1; Matthew 10:7–23; Luke 21:32)
- is delayed (e.g., Matthew 25:1–13; Luke 19:11–27)

Though these statements seem contradictory, they actually describe the mystery of the faith in which there is a delayed

---

7. Additional information on the different political and religious views of the kingdom of God challenged by Jesus can be found in chapters 7 and 9 of my book *The Here and Not Yet*.

8. Medearis, *Speaking of Jesus*, 155.

Allegiance to the King

element to the coming of kingdom of God, with it being inaugurated but not consummated. Baptist theologian George Eldon Ladd described this eschatological tension as the time when the "Kingdom of God which is yet to come in power and great glory is actually present among men in advance in an unexpected form to bring to men in the present evil Age the blessings of The Age to Come."[9] Hence we can say that active rule and reign of the Creator King is here today just as much as it is coming and will one day be here.

Though the siren call of certainty begs us to explain away the mystery and the paradox of the inaugurated eschatological tension of the kingdom of God, the way of the mystery directs us to embrace the tension. The way in which the Creator "expresses His natural hiddenness," St. Maximos reminds us, "makes it the more hidden through the revelation."[10] Accordingly, though we may not fully understand the mysterious movements of the Creator, we are to embrace the paradoxical message of Jesus about the arrival of the kingdom of God.

The Enthroned King

Writing a few decades after Jesus, the apostle Paul would summarize the message of Jesus in terms of "incarnation and enthronement."[11] Jesus was the promised one about whom the prophets had foretold. Furthermore, he was also the incarnated Creator King of heaven and earth, who entered into the world through "David's seed in terms of flesh" (Romans 1:3, NTfE). While this statement itself is powerful, Paul goes to say that Jesus was resurrected from the dead and enthroned as "the King, our Lord" (Romans 1:4, NTfE).

The enthronement of Jesus as the King of heaven and earth can be seen most clearly in the first chapter of Acts. After giving his followers some last-minute instructions, Jesus is lifted up into

---

9. Ladd, *Gospel of the Kingdom*, 55.
10. Maximos, *Various Texts*, 166.
11. Bates, *Salvation by Allegiance Alone*, 30–34.

the skies and hidden from sight by a cloud (Acts 1:9). This action harkens back to Daniel 7:13–14 (NIV), in which "one like a son of man" approaches the Ancient of Days with "clouds of heaven" and is enthroned with "all nations and peoples of every language" worshiping him. Jesus, the Son of Man, as he commonly called himself (e.g., Matthew 9:6; Mark 8:38; John 8:28), is now the "true world ruler, with all the warring pagan nations made subject to him."[12]

Though we don't think much about such language, for Paul to say that Jesus is the "blessed and only Sovereign, the King of kings and Lord of lords" (1 Timothy 6:15, ESV) is to effectively commit treason against the Roman Empire and its divine ruler. Starting in the days of Caesar Augustus (63 BCE–14 CE), the emperors of the land were seen as divine gods, with temples dedicated to their worship being built across the empire from Spain to Judea. Accordingly, for Paul to claim that Jesus of Nazareth was the Creator God and the true King of the earth was to effectively deny the exclusive rule of the Caesars (e.g., Acts 17:6–8). Later followers of Jesus would face death at the hands of Roman authorities for upholding these claims as they refused to renounce their loyalty to Jesus and offer sacrifices to the human emperor of the land.

Pledging our undivided allegiance to Jesus doesn't mean, however, that we can't be proud of our nation, religion, or holy book. Paul, for example, was a Roman citizen who obeyed the laws of the land even though he disagreed with common worship practices of the day (e.g., Acts 16:37–38; 22:25–29; Romans 13:1–7). He also was proud of his Jewish heritage and the Scriptures of his youth even if he now reinterpreted them through the lens of Jesus the Messiah (e.g., Acts 22:3–21; Philippians 3:2–11). As Paul's life shows us, following Jesus means that our first allegiance is to Jesus, our King and Lord. We are first and foremost disciples of Jesus before we are citizens of a nation, followers of a religion, and/or readers of a holy book. If ever there is a disagreement or test of loyalty between these things, may we echo words of Simon Peter and the apostles as they stood before the same assembly who tortured

---

12. Wright, *Simply Jesus*, 196.

Allegiance to the King

and killed Jesus a few weeks previously: "We must obey God, not human beings!" (Acts 5:29, NTfE).

Exchange of Sovereignties

Lest we forget, claiming Jesus as our Lord and King goes beyond giving him priority over our country, religion, and holy book. There is a very real, albeit unseen, transfer of allegiance that happens when we bow our knees to the risen King and call upon him to rescue us (e.g., Romans 10:9–13; Colossians 1:12–13). At that precise moment in time we are "delivered from Satan's kingdom and catapulted into the kingdom of God"[13] as describe by Vineyard pastor theologian Don Williams. No longer are we bound by the chains of sin, addictions, pain, sorrow, death, and evil. We are now children of the Living God, joint heirs with Jesus the Messiah (e.g., Romans 8:17; Galatians 4:4–7).

Though unseen, and sometimes even unfelt, this spiritual exchange of sovereignties is at the core of the good news of Jesus. Throughout the Scriptures there is a paradox where the Creator God is described as both the current King and the coming King of the world. This paradox is set against the backdrop of a battle being raged across the visible and invisible dimensions of creation between the forces of evil and the Lord Almighty. Though the origin of this war is shrouded in mystery, with the Scriptures being silent on the details that we so desperately crave, pastor theologian Gregory Boyd reminds us that the biblical authors understood that fighting against "such things as injustice, oppression, greed, and apathy toward the needy was to participate directly or indirectly in a cosmic war that had engulfed the earth."[14]

Accordingly, the choice to follow Jesus is also a choice *not* to follow the ways of the evil one. Hence the early followers of Jesus understood that the "one who professed in response to the gospel, 'I believe,' was the one who said simultaneously: 'I renounce

---

13. D. Williams, *Start Here*, 7.
14. Boyd, *God at War*, 14.

you Satan, your pomp, your service, your works' (Chrysostom); 'I renounce the devil and his work, this age and its pleasure' (Ambrose)."[15] Don Williams elaborates on this exchange of sovereignties in declaring that:

> To say, "Jesus is Lord" means to renounce all other lords. No ideology, political philosophy, drug or person can have a higher claim on our lives. All our idols must be pulled down, repented of and crushed at Jesus' feet. The idols of pride, power, control, self-medication, family, friends, illicit sex, internet pornography, legalism, self-righteousness, mind-altering meditation, witchcraft, magic, cults, gambling, work, self-advancement, children, health, and security in old age must go. Anything that takes the place of Jesus in our hearts, in our passions and in our devotion is an idol. As Elijah the prophet said to the nation of Israel, "How long will you waver between two opinions? If the Lord is God, follow him" (1 Kings 18:21). God has called us and revealed Jesus as Lord to us. Follow Him![16]

Water Baptism

Throughout church history water baptism has served as a symbol of this sovereignty exchange. In a mysterious way that no one fully understands, the act being immersed in water connects us with Jesus' death and resurrection (e.g., Romans 6; Colossians 2:9–15). As we go into the waters, we are set free from the rule of the evil by "dying" with Jesus (Romans 7:1–6). In coming up once again, we join Jesus in his resurrection—becoming, in essence, a new creation who, by God's grace, can offer our allegiance to the true King.

Jesus' own baptism in the River Jordan carries within it echoes of this spiritual exchange of sovereignty along with a denial of the right of his religion and nationality to determine his path. As a first-century Israelite, Jesus would have grown up learning about

---

15. Hinlicky, *Beloved Community*, 221.
16. D. Williams, *Start Here*, 16–17.

the Abrahamic covenant and the election of the Jews as the people of God. Those outside of Judaism (e.g., the Gentiles) could become a member of God's people by being baptized and submitting to the laws of the religion. Jesus' cousin John the Baptist challenged this view by declaring that descendants of Abraham must themselves be baptized in a "public act of repentance and purification in hopes of forgiveness on the impending day of the Lord."[17] In presenting himself to be baptized, Jesus embraced John's message that religion or ethnicity alone isn't enough to gain the favor of the Creator.

As Jesus rose from the water that day, the Holy Spirit descended upon Jesus in the likeness of a dove while the voice of God the Father confirmed his pleasure in Jesus (Matthew 3:16–17; Mark 1:10–11; Luke 3:22; John 1:32–34). This is the first time in the Scriptures that we see the Trinity together at the same place at the same time. It is also the only time that the dove is used to symbolize the Spirit. To understand the importance of this, we must realize that the symbol of the Roman Empire was the eagle, which was also closely connected to the god Jupiter, who was the chief deity of Rome. When a new emperor was crowned, the people would watch the birds for a sign from the gods. If the bird of prey landed upon the shoulder of a man, that man would be considered blessed by the gods and become the new king and emperor of Rome.[18] First-century hearers of the story of Jesus' baptism would have recognized the cultural significance of the dove and understood it as a declaration that Jesus, not Caesar, was King.[19]

---

17. Hinlicky, *Beloved Community*, 229.

18. Street, *Heaven on Earth*, 77.

19. It is also worth noting that the dove is a prey bird whereas the eagle is a predatory bird. This highlights the upside-down kingdom of Jesus, which is marked by love, gentleness, forgiveness, peace, and mercy, as opposed to the Roman Empire, which is marked by the sword, death, power, and brute force. Jesus followers in the United States of America should take note of this symbolism as the country was modeled after the Roman Republic with the eagle being chosen as the national symbol. Brian Zahnd's book *A Farewell to Mars* and Greg Boyd's *The Myth of a Christian Nation* are two recommended books for American Christians.

Accordingly, when we follow Jesus' example in being baptized, we are in effect acting out our own death and declaring that our nation, religion, and holy book no longer has a hold on us. We are now members of a new kingdom under a new King whose citizens span the globe and the course of history. We are, as John the Revelator said, part of a "great multitude that no one could count, from every nation, tribe, people and language, standing before the throne and before the Lamb" (Revelation 7:9, NIV).

— 6 —

Salvation in Motion

Trusting God with all our hearts is a complete surrender, a life decision to be in all the time rather than relying on our own "insight," our ability to understand, to fathom, to solve, to figure out. Trust remains when our reason betrays us, when we don't understand the mysteries of God and faith, when we don't see what God is up to—including when God for all intents and purposes is not faithful or trustworthy.

—PETER ENNS[1]

MY FIRST JOB AFTER college was working for the U. S. Bureau of Land Management helping map the off-road 4x4, dirt bike, and ATV trails in the high mountain desert of the Northern Paiute people located in southwest Idaho. Each day I would mount a GPS unit on a dirt bike and take off, verifying the condition of known trails while recording the location of new trails. It was, as I'm sure you are thinking, a great job as I got paid to ride a motorcycle through some of the most beautiful and remote areas of the lower forty-eight states.

At times the trails would make use of the old dry creek beds scattered across the area. These creek beds were full of loose sand

---

1. Enns, *Sin of Certainty*, 104.

washed there by the occasional spring flood caused by snowmelt. Though it may sound prudent to slow down before riding out into the loose sand of these beds, I quickly learned to do the opposite. Going slow would cause the wheels of the motorcycle to bog down and get stuck. Going fast, however, allowed the bike to skim over the top of the loose sand. And strangely enough, it granted me more control of the bike as the wheels weren't getting stuck in the loose sand.

Following Jesus into the darkness of the unknown is similar to driving on those old dry creek beds. If we go slow, trying to maintain control over our own lives while feeling our way forward, we will ultimately fall prey to the cares of this world, which seek to choke us out. The only safe way forward, contrary to popular belief, is to give up everything and throw ourselves into the way of Jesus. And though it may initially be disconcerting, in doing so we will find safety and peace as we navigate the hazards of life.

Forward Movement

When Jesus of Nazareth started his teaching ministry, he was just another Jewish teacher in the land. Later on, as people started to realize that his message was different than the other teachers, they struggled to find a term to adequately describe their new life. As the years went by, the term they choose to embrace was "the Way" (Acts 9:2; 19:9; 19:23). Some of their neighbors, however, had a hard time understanding this phrase so they called them "Christians" (Acts 11:26). Though the terms are different, buried deep within both is the concept of motion or movement.

The phrase "the Way" carries within itself the idea of moving towards something while emphasizes the concept that there is certain manner in which one is to be moving. Hence, we can talk about a "way of life" or the "way to do something." Closely connected to this self-designation is the idea of being a pilgrim, in that we are people, as pastor and theologian Eugene Peterson declared, "who spend our lives going someplace, going to God, and whose

Salvation in Motion

path for getting there is the way, Jesus Christ."[2] Our lives, as such, are to be lived with a measure of discontentment, for we know that we have not yet arrived, both on a personal emotional/spiritual level as well as in a physical sense. Being a pilgrim of the Way means, therefore, that we are constantly being transformed into the image of Jesus (2 Corinthians 3:18) through the grace of God while looking forward to the restored heaven and earth, where there will be no more sorrow, pain, or death (Revelation 21).

Though we tend to forget about it, the Greek word normally translated as "Christian" (Χριστιανός) in English literally means "little Christ," which can be further defined as "follower of Christ."[3] Hence it is a term that emphasizes movement, as being a follower of someone suggests that we are active adherents or disciples of that person. As disciples of Jesus we are, to quote Eugene Peterson again, "people who spend our lives apprenticed to our master, Jesus Christ" in an ever "growing-learning relationship."[4] We are to be so in love with Jesus that we seek to emulate him in every thought and deed. As St. Maximos wrote, "he who loves Christ is bound to imitate Him to the best of his ability."[5]

Philosopher James K. A. Smith builds on this concept in declaring that "being a disciple of Jesus is not primarily a matter of getting the right ideas and doctrines and beliefs into your head in order to guarantee proper behavior; rather, it's a matter of being the kind of person who loves rightly—who loves God and neighbor and is oriented to the world by the primacy of that love."[6] Hence to embrace being a Christian is to radically change the manner in which we engage the world around us while moving beyond simple answers of certainty. It is to put our hands into the hands of Jesus and trust him as we walk into the darkness of the unknown.

Movement is the one thread that runs throughout all these terms. To be a member of the Way is to embrace a new way of

2. Peterson, *Long Obedience*, 17.
3. Perschbacher, *New Analytical Greek Lexicon*, 440.
4. Peterson, *Long Obedience*, 17.
5. Maximos, *Four Hundred Texts*, 107.
6. Smith, *Desiring the Kingdom*, 32–33.

life whereas to be a Christian is to be a follower of Christ. Being a disciple means emulating Jesus while being a pilgrim entails being on a journey with Jesus. The concept of movement is buried deep within the core of Christianity. In reflecting on this, Bishop Kallistos Ware declared that "Christianity is more than a theory about the universe, more than teachings written down on paper; it is a path along which we journey—in the deepest and richest sense, the way of life."[7]

Eyes on the Way

The problem with riding across dry creek beds is that there are usually objects half-buried in the sand. As long as I continued to focus on where I was going, I tended to avoid these obstacles as I skimmed across the loose sand. However, there were times when fear caused me to shift my eyes off the path and onto the obstacles themselves. When that happened, I would invariably slow down, causing the sand to swallow my wheels. In so many words, I would crash—falling over onto whatever obstacle I was trying to avoid. The same thing happens in our lives when we shift our focus from forward movement with Jesus to past moments of certainty.

Over the years, well-meaning theologians and thinkers across the spectrum and history of Christianity have sought to bring clarity to the dynamic nature of salvation. They have done this by reducing the mystery of movement into a set order of salvation moments.[8] People are saved, they say, the moment they recite this prayer, do this action, don't do this, or any combination thereof. The Scriptures themselves, however, don't offer us a set list of moments in our journey. Similar to how the kingdom of God is here, is coming, and will one day be here, our salvation is one of mysterious inaugurated tension. Through the life, death, resurrection, and ascension of Jesus, we have been saved (e.g., Ephesians 1:13; 1 Corinthians 1:21; Titus 3:3–7), are being saved (e.g., 1 Corinthians

---

7. Ware, *Orthodox Way*, 7–8.
8. Howard, *Brazos Introduction*, 247–54.

1:18; Philippians 2:12–13; Hebrews 10:39), and will one day be saved (e.g., 1 John 3:2; Romans 5:9; Philippians 3:20–21). Hence we must, as Matthew Bates warns, "be wary of quick answers that harmonize the multiple images pertaining to salvation (and their complex past, present, and future aspects) by offering a rigid order of salvation."[9]

Jesus' invitation to follow him is more than just a single moment in time. It is an ongoing invitation to be "transformed into his [Jesus] image with ever-increasing glory" (2 Corinthians 3:18, NIV) or, as pastor Rick Williams puts it, to "become a different kind of person—a transformed person."[10] It is an invitation into the mystery and paradox of salvation in which we encounter the living God in the unpredictability of life. To have all the right answers and the easy fixes to our salvation is to remove the mystery and the paradox from life. "And if," to quote spiritual formation professor M. Robert Mulholland, "there is no room for mystery there is no room for God, because God is the ultimate mystery."[11]

Keeping our eyes focused on a lifetime of movement rather than on rigid moments of salvation requires trust. We have to trust that the Creator King really loves us and is actively involved in our lives. In order for us to truly trust Jesus, we have to let go of our fear of the unknown and our desire for certainty. We have to come to the point, as M. Robert Mulholland says, where we "let go of our limited concept of God . . . and . . . allow God to be whatever God wants to be in our life."[12] When we do this, we find ourselves drawn forward by the Spirit through the ups and downs of life. The obstacles are still there; it is just that our eyes are focused forward on the Way and not on the moments. We, in fact, come to the point where we embrace the mysteries and uncertainties that move throughout our lives as normal parts of the Way and opportunities to trust our Beloved more deeply.[13]

9. Bates, *Salvation by Allegiance Alone*, 35.
10. R. Williams, *Uncomfortable Growth*, 64–65.
11. Mulholland, *Invitation to a Journey*, 173.
12. Mulholland, *Invitation to a Journey*, 173.
13. Enns, *Sin of Certainty*, 205.

Part 2: The Way

Dancing with Moments

Years ago, another Joshua crossed a dry creek bed in the desert—or I should say a "dry riverbed." This Joshua was the leader of the people of Israel and he was following the Creator King across the Jordan River into the promised land. As the story goes, the Lord told him to have twelve men pick up twelve stones from the middle of the riverbed and stack them on the riverbank (Joshua 4:1–9). These stones were to serve as monument to the people reminding them of what God had done that day. And while crossing the Jordan River on dry ground was an important moment in the history of the Israelites, they weren't supposed to stay next to the stones for the rest of their lives. Rather they had to trust the Lord and follow him into the uncertain future of entering a strange and hostile land.

As the years went by those twelve stones reminded the people of the moment the Lord saved them by parting the Jordan River. The people would also remember other moments in their salvation journey from Egypt to the land that would become their home. These moments served as guideposts for them as they journeyed into the unknown darkness of the future. In a sense, the people of Israel embarked on a dance with the different moments in their history. Locking hands with the salvation experience of leaving Egypt, they picked up their feet and swirled around with the purging of the desert crossing and dipped low with the moment they entered the land of milk and honey through the waters of the Jordan. Spinning and twisting together, these historical salvation moments merged with the living salvation moments of the people till only the blur of the dance remained.

We join this same dance of the Way when we answer the call of Jesus and allow the living and historical moments of our inaugurated atonement to swirl around and through us. We were saved along with all of humanity and creation at that gloriously dark moment on Golgotha when the Son of Man breathed his last. We were also saved the moment we bowed our knees and pledged our loyalties to King Jesus. The dance increases in speed and complexity as the Spirit weaves in living moments of salvation from today and

Salvation in Motion

tomorrow. And in the great paradoxical mystery of the Creator, the moment we stand before the throne of Christ intermingles throughout this dance of salvation.

In reflecting on this dance of moments, we must come to realization that our salvation, as Father Anthony M. Coniaris of the Eastern Orthodox Church notes, "is not static but dynamic; it is not a completed state, a state of having arrived, a state of having made it, but a constant moving toward theosis, toward becoming like Christ, toward receiving the fullness of God's life."[14] It is like driving out onto the loose sand of those dry creek beds in that we are to continue to move forward rather than trying to stop or slow down. Though it can be hard, we are to keep moving forward through the fears and the unknown fog of life, knowing that we are dancing with the One who knows and loves us beyond our imagination. As the unknown author of Hebrews said, "let us throw off everything that hinders and the sin that so easily entangles. And let us run with perseverance the race marked out for us fixing our eyes on Jesus, the pioneer and perfecter of faith" (Hebrews 12:1–2, NIV).

---

14. Coniaris, *Introducing the Orthodox Church*, 48.

— 7 —

Doing What Jesus Did

The claim I believe in God is nothing but a lie if it is not manifest in our lives, because one only believes in God insofar as one loves.

—PETER ROLLINS[1]

He who relies on theoretical knowledge alone is not yet a faithful servant: a faithful servant is one who expresses his faith in Christ through obedience to His commandments.

—ST. MARK THE ASCETIC[2]

THERE WERE ABOUT A dozen of us sitting around the restaurant table that evening. We were five years into starting a new church and were having an identity crisis. Though we had seen God do some great things in our small rural community over the course of those years, we also had been through three senior pastors. We had loved each of them dearly and embraced each of their visions for our small church during their short time with us. And while we understood the economic and medical reasons as to

1. Rollins, *Insurrection*, 127.
2. Mark, *On Those who Think*, 125.

why these bivocational pastors had to leave, the rotating nature of their departures left us emotionally drained and in search of a reason to continue.

Hence, we were sitting at that table that night talking about the future our church. Overwhelmingly we all wanted to continue moving forward with the grand experiment; however, we also didn't want to just *do* church, we wanted to *be* the church. We wanted to continue helping feed the hungry and clothe those in need through our food pantry and clothing closet. And while we loved good Bible teaching, we also wanted to embrace the dancing hand of the Spirit, who would draw us deeper into a relationship with the Creator while healing the sick, giving us visions, and challenging our paradigms.

At some point during our conversation, the moto "doing what Jesus did"[3] was suggested to the group. As we sat there pondering that phrase, we realized that it really did capture our heart. We desperately wanted to join Jesus on his mission to transform our community by doing the things that the Scriptures said he did. In other words, we wanted to preach the message of the kingdom of God, love people of all backgrounds and social standings, heal the sick, cleanse the lepers, raise the dead, cast out demons, and love God with our whole heart, mind, strength, and soul (e.g., Matthew 10:7–8; 22:37–40).

Imitators of Jesus

Though it is a lot of work, I love being the father of three crazy fun-loving boys. One of the coolest and most humbling parts of being a father is watching them try to be like me. Every day they watch me and then try to copy what I do—from the way I walk to the

---

3. Though I don't recall the exact date of this supper meeting, I know it happened in the early part of 2011 (i.e., February–April). A few years after the church embraced the "Doing what Jesus did" moto, Robby Dawkins released a book entitled *Do What Jesus Did* (June 2013), which explored the same concept. Neither one of us knew the other had independently stumbled upon the phrase, though we both were part of the wider Vineyard USA church family.

manner in which I shrug my shoulders to the words that come out of my mouth. Imitation is, after all, the way in which we all learn. Babies watch and copy their parents, kids copy those who are older than them, and adults imitate their friends and those who they respect.

Yet for some reason it is considered taboo to think that we can imitate the way of life modeled by Jesus of Nazareth. Instead the wider church culture tells us that Jesus is the one exception to the rule of imitation. The things he did, we are told, are one-off events that are never again to be repeated in human history. In some ways this claim is correct in that Jesus is the Creator King himself, who entered human history to break the rule of the evil one and usher in the kingdom of God through his life, death, resurrection, and ascension. At the same time the claim that we are not supposed to imitate Jesus is very wrong and goes against the entire thrust of the Scriptures.

The four historical narratives of Jesus' life and ministry (i.e., the Gospel According to Matthew, Mark, Luke, and John) were written for two reasons. The first is to inform us of what happened when the Creator himself came down and dwelled among us. We, the followers of Jesus, are able to live a life of freedom from evil because of Jesus; hence we needed to know what happened. The second reason the Gospels were written flows from the first in that the narratives were written to help teach us how we are to live our lives. We are, in effect, supposed to imitate Jesus in all things as he is the truest representation of humanity. This is why the apostle Paul told the church in Corinth to "be imitators of me, as I am of Christ" (1 Corinthians 11:1, ESV).

The call to imitate Jesus can be seen the clearest in the writings of Luke the Evangelist. Drawing on eyewitness accounts, Luke tells us all about the message and actions of Jesus before showing us how Jesus taught, trained, and released the twelve apostles and the seventy-two disciples to proclaim the same message while doing the same actions as he had done (Luke 9:1–2; 10:1–20). Later on, after Jesus' death and resurrection, we see the Twelve doing it all again (Acts 5:12–16), followed by Stephen (Acts 6:8–10), and

Philip the Evangelist (Acts 8:5–8) before being passed on to the apostle Paul (Acts 19:11–12). St. Luke even tells us that Stephen imitated Jesus in the manner of his death in that they both forgave their murderers during the act itself (Luke 23:34; Acts 7:60).

Writing a few decades after Luke and Paul, John the son of Zebedee builds upon their encouragement to imitate Jesus. In the second chapter of his first letter, John states that "if someone claims, 'I know him [Jesus] well!' but doesn't keep his commandments, he's obviously a liar. His life doesn't match his words. But the one who keeps God's word is the person in whom we see God's mature love. This is the only way to be sure we're in God. *Anyone who claims to be intimate with God ought to live the same kind of life Jesus lived*" (1 John 2:4–6, MSG, emphasis added). In a nutshell, if we truly are followers of Jesus, then we must imitate him by "doing what Jesus did."

Lovers of the Creator

It was Jesus' last night with his disciples before his betrayal and death. Sitting in the upper room, he tries to prepare his followers for the grief and pain that is to come. As he looks over the faces of the remaining eleven apostles (Judas Iscariot having since departed), Jesus repeatedly encourages them to stay on the path and keep doing the things he had commanded them to do: "Anyone who loves me will obey my teaching. My Father will love them, and we will come to them and make our home with them. Anyone who does not love me will not obey my teaching. These words you hear are not my own; they belong to the Father who sent me" (John 14:23–24, NIV; e.g., John 14:12, 15, 21; 15:10, 14).

In reflecting on these instructions along with Jesus' previous commandment for his followers to love one another (John 15:12) and obey his commandments (John 14:15, 23), St. Maximos states that "he who does not love his neighbor fails to keep the commandment, and so cannot love the Lord."[4] In other words, to love Jesus

---

4. Maximos, *Four Hundred Texts*, 54.

is to obey Jesus. There is something that happens to us when we bow our knees to Jesus and pledge our allegiance to him that makes us want to obey his commands. It is not that we are trying to earn anything from him, but rather it is out of pure love for him that we are motivated to obey him. "Love is the fulfillment of the law," Dr. Beth Stovell of Ambrose Seminary explains: "love is seen through compassion to others, love is shown in deeds and we do deeds because of love, love is a gift from God, love is serving in good-will without self-interest, love creates harmony and makes us children of God, and love is modeled by Jesus, who is a great leader of the faith."[5] It is in this vein that St. Maximos wrote his *Four Hundred Texts on Love* to show us how to live out the love of Jesus, for a man who loves God "naturally strives to confirm to His will."[6]

There is a mysterious paradox at work here. We come to Jesus having nothing and unable to do anything beyond falling at his feet. In this act of total surrender, Jesus picks us up and loves us unconditionally as we are. Dusting off the slime and dirt, he tells us everything he has learned from the Father and invites us to join him in his mission to redeem all of creation (John 15:14–17). We, out of love for him, then choose to embark on a lifelong journey of doing the things he did. It is as the Pilgrim said to the Forester in the anonymously written nineteenth-century Russian work *The Way of The Pilgrim*:

> According to the holy Fathers, one who performs saving works simply from the fear of hell follows the way of bondage, and he who does the same just in order to be rewarded with the kingdom of heaven follows the path of a bargainer with God. The one they call a slave, the other a hireling. But God wants us to come to Him as sons to their Father; He wants us to behave ourselves honorable from love for Him and zeal for His service; He wants us to find our happiness in uniting ourselves with Him in a saving union of mind and heart.[7]

---

5. Stovell, "Love One Another," 426.
6. Maximos, *Four Hundred Texts*, 84.
7. French, trans., *Way of the Pilgrim*, 34.

Doing What Jesus Did

This idea that we are the children (daughters and sons) of God is something repeated throughout the New Testament (e.g., 1 John 3:1; Galatians 3:26; John 1:12; Romans 8:16). Yes, there is a sense in which he is our King and we are his subjects; but even in that relationship there is a deeper truth that all of humanity was originally created to be the children of God. And as children, the Creator desperately longs for us to follow and obey him out of love and respect rather than fear or bondage. Jesus' words to his followers in the upper room are in essence similar to the words of all parents to their children: "My child, please, out of the love you have for me, don't go to that party and get drunk on alcohol or take illegal drugs. Rather, come with me and learn how to live a life of freedom and love."

Jesus, therefore, is asking us, his daughters and sons, to follow and obey him not out fear of punishment or for hope of reward, but because we love him. The shift from slave or hireling to a child of the Most High is a very important shift that changes everything. Serving God as a slave or a hireling will only lead to frustration and pain whereas the actions of a child who loves his Father know no boundaries.

Moving beyond Believing

St. James the Just, the brother of Jesus, famously remarked that while it is good to believe that there is one God, it isn't enough to simply believe. "Faith by itself," James wrote, "if it is not accompanied by action, is dead" (James 2:17, NIV). The intellectual act of believing something doesn't necessary mean that our life will be affected, or our actions changed. Demons themselves, after all, believe in God Almighty while still pursuing the path of destruction (James 2:19). No, if we truly desire to walk the path of Jesus, we must move beyond believing to something more. Philosopher and theologian Peter Rollins pondered this dilemma in his book *Insurrection: To Believe Is Human; To Doubt, Divine*:

Part 2: The Way

> The empirical rendering of the question [Do you believe in God?] may continue to interest the philosopher and it is no doubt a fascinating conversation to have with friends over a drink. But it is not a specifically theological question when taken in this way. For the believer who passes through the Christian experience, God is no longer related to as an object *out there*. Rather, God is affirmed only through a passionate participation in life itself.
>
> This means that we can no longer claim that we know God while hating our neighbor. Those who have taken part in the event of Conversion (participation in Crucifixion and Resurrection) cannot claim to believe in God except insofar as love emanates from them, transforming the world within which they are embedded.[8]

Moving beyond simply believing in God means allowing that belief to transform who we are and what we do. "The mystery of our salvation," St. Maximos tells us, "informs our way of life with intelligence and makes intelligence the glory of our way of life. It turns our practice of the virtues into contemplation manifest in terms of action, and our contemplation into divinely initiated practice."[9] We can, if we want to, stop the love of God from permeating our lives. We can hold this love at bay, taking it out on Sunday mornings or when it benefits us. Jesus, however, did not die on the cross just so we can say we believe in him. He died so that we can join with him in transforming the world and destroying the works of sin, evil, and death. We have been set free and given a mission to love people. As St. Maximos once said, "the person who loves God cannot help loving every man as himself."[10]

---

8. Peter Rollins, *Insurrection*, 127. Emphasis original.
9. Maximos, *Various Texts*, 257.
10. Maximos, *Four Hundred Texts*, 54.

PART 3

The Journey

By faith Abraham obeyed when he was called to go out to a place that he was to receive as an inheritance. And he went out, not knowing where he was going.

—ANONYMOUS[1]

To be a Christian is to be a traveler. Our situation, say the Greek Fathers, is like that of the Israelite people in the desert of Sinai: we live in tents, not houses, for spiritually we are always on the move. We are on a journey through the inward space of the heart, a journey not measured by the hours of our watch or the days of the calendar, for it is a journey of time into eternity.

—BISHOP KALLISTOS WARE[2]

---

1. Hebrews 11:8, ESV
2. Ware, *Orthodox Way*, 7.

— **8** —

On the Path

And if we answer the call to discipleship, where will it lead us?
What decisions and partings will it demand? To answer this
question, we shall have to go to him, for only he knows the answer.
Only Jesus Christ, who bids us follow him, knows the journey's end.
But we do know that it will be a road of boundless mercy.
Discipleship means joy.

—DIETRICH BONHOEFFER[1]

WITH EACH FOOTFALL MY body was propelled deeper into the Upper Kiamichi River Wilderness of southeast Oklahoma within the Choctaw Nation. Having cut my teeth reading the western stories of Louis L'Amour, I had dreamed for years about hiking deep into untamed lands of North America without having the need to turn around and return to civilization. And on that day the dream was coming true. I was heading into the wilderness carrying everything I needed to survive for two days on my back.

My wife and at least one of our other two companions, on the other hand, weren't quite as thrilled about the experience as I was. For some reason they did not embrace the thirty-plus pounds of

---

1. Bonhoeffer, *Cost of Discipleship*, 38.

weight we each were carrying, nor did they revel in the light drizzle of rain that accompanied us that weekend. Rather they seemed to drag slower and slower with each step, stopping and resting every few minutes. While at first these delays didn't bother me, I soon found myself getting angry at my slower companions. I was having the time of my life and I wanted to see what was around the next corner or over the next hill. Stopping and waiting for others seemed like a huge imposition.

Over the next decade and a half, the three miles of that original trip turned into thirty while the wilderness became more remote. Having since moved to Idaho, I have had the pleasure of hiking deep into the Sawtooth Wilderness and fishing the backcountry lakes of the Frank Church River of No Return Wilderness (both located within the traditional lands of the Shoshone-Bannock Nation) as well as circling the Seven Devils Mountains in the Hells Canyon Wilderness on traditional Nimiipuu (Nez Perce) land. One thing I learned through all these trips is that no two people will hike at the same speed for any length of time. Though everyone is on the same trail, someone will eventually drop back while another will move forward to take the point. Rather than getting upset at folks, like I did during that first backpacking trip, I have learned to embrace the different speeds of people—knowing that eventually we will all arrive at our intended destination.

Learning to Walk

When I first started backpacking, I didn't think much about the way in which I walked. After all, I had been walking for decades before that first wet trip into the Oklahoma wilderness. The more trips I went on, however, the more I realized that the way I walked before wasn't sustainable. If I wanted to continue backpacking, I had to change the way in which I walked.

Checking some books out of the library, I started to read about how to backpack. These books not only helped me revamp my gear (e.g., backpack, boots, clothes, etc.), they also taught me how to walk. For example, one of the books taught me about the rest step, which is a type of step that helps the leg muscles rest for a split second between each step, thereby reducing leg fatigue. It also taught me how to walk up a slope using my entire foot rather than just my toes. Another book encouraged me to slow down and enjoy the trail itself rather than always trying to push on to the next curve or to crest the next hill. As I put into practice these lessons gleaned from those who went before me, the way in which I walked began to change. I began to see and experience things on the trail that I used to miss. My steps became more deliberate and focused as I relaxed and let the trail lead me rather than trying to conquer the trail.

In a similar way, when we embark on the path of the Creator into the unknown, we must relearn how to walk. The way in which we were taught previously will not work as the path we take is different than that which we have formerly traveled. Rather than pushing onward, we are to become like little children learning to walk anew. Sadly, most of us tend to want to skip past the relearning stages and focus instead on the excellency that comes afterward. Psychologist Angela Duckworth once noted that our tendency to "prefer our excellence fully formed"[2] can be seen in the way we view someone who is truly good at something—whether that be a professional athlete, movie actress/actor, musician, business leader, or someone full of compassion and mercy. Though these people have spent countless hours practicing the small and mundane parts of their craft, we choose to focus on the moment or moments when they were at the top of their game. We embrace this myth of fully formed excellence because we want to believe that we can somehow obtain greatness without the pain, toil, and self-discipline that is truly required.

Walking into the darkness of the unknown with the Breath of Life requires us to give up this myth and to embrace the intentional journey of spiritual formation through which we become more Christlike. As M. Robert Mulholland says, "the way to spiritual wholeness is seen to lie in an increasingly faithful response to the One whose purpose shapes our path, whose grace redeems

---

2. Duckworth, *Grit*, 39.

our detours, whose power liberates us from crippling bondages of the prior journey and whose transformation presence meets us at each turn of the road. In other words, holistic spirituality is a pilgrimage of deepening responsiveness to God's control of our life and being."[3]

It is in the mundane practice of that which is small that we really see God. It is when we choose to love the unlovable, to pause before we act, to hold our tongues, or the countless other little, vastly overlooked actions we do each day, that we truly become followers of Jesus. Each moment, no matter how small, when coupled with the grace of God, becomes a training ground for our muscles. Slowly over time, our spiritual muscles begin to react in a manner that is wholly different than they once did. We are being transformed, to reference St. Paul, "into his [Jesus] image with ever-increasing glory, which comes from the Lord, who is the Spirit" (2 Corinthians 3:18, NIV). The beauty of this is that the more we train our muscles (spiritual or physical), the easier it becomes to walk anew. Soon, without any effort from us, the loving mother of the grace of God causes our souls, in the words of St. John of the Cross, to "find sweet and pleasant spiritual milk in everything belonging to God and great delight in spiritual exercises, because now God gives her [our souls] his breast of tender love."[4]

Traveling at Different Speeds

A few years ago, I attended a Good Friday service in a late-1800s frontier penitentiary that had been turned into a museum. After a short drama skit and a sermonette, a few hundred of us headed out on a 1.6-mile hike to the top of a local butte crowned with a huge cross.[5] As I left the penitentiary, I stopped to pick up a

---

3. Mulholland, *Invitation to a Journey*, 16.
4. John of the Cross, *Dark Night*, 8–9.
5. The service was put on by the Vineyard Boise Christian Fellowship (Boise, Idaho) and was held at the Old Idaho Penitentiary, which was built in 1872. The hike was from the Old Penitentiary to the top of Table Rock, a local landmark that hosts a cross that can be seen day and night from various

small pebble, which became a symbol of the burdens I carry every day. With each step I invited the Spirit of the Living King to invade my life, breathing in his life and will while breathing out my own. When I reached the top of the butte, I gently laid the stone at the foot of the cross before adding my voice to the growing chorus worshiping the crucified Messiah. As you can imagine, the symbolism of such a service was amazing—transforming a well-known story into something more real.

In reflecting on that evening, there was one moment on the hike that stands above the rest. About half a mile from the trailhead, the path tops a small ridge that gives one a panoramic view of the butte. Being in a high desert, there are no trees along the path, just sagebrush and rocks. When standing on that ridge, you can see the entire trail winding up the butte with people scattered out along the path. Some of them are running up the mountain, while others are walking slowly with small children. A few are clumped in groups, talking and laughing, while some are walking by themselves in deep meditation. Though we were all walking along the same path headed to the same destination, each of our journeys was different.

In a similar way, each of our journeys along the Way of Jesus are different though we walk with the same Spirit along the same path towards the same destination. St. Maximos the Confessor puts it this way: "God reveals himself to each person according to each person's mode of conceiving Him."[6] This is the definition of a multifaceted spiritual formation journey in which we embrace the mystery of not knowing while understanding that our path towards Jesus is one of movement and love. Though the siren call of our culture tries to convince us that our journey is (or must be) the same as that of our sisters and brothers, the mystery reminds us that we do not know the fullness of the Spirit's work within and among our fellow travelers. "The points of common ground with God," Evan Howard reminds us, "will vary from person to person.

---

locations in Boise.

6. Maximos, *Various Texts*, 186.

Different areas of human experience become the doorways of God's transforming work."[7]

Multifaceted

M. Robert Mulholland defines spiritual formation as "the process of being formed in the image of Christ for the sake of others."[8] This definition fits nicely with the Way of life discussed in the previous section, in which following Jesus of Nazareth is a movement towards the Creator with an outpouring of love towards our follow journeyers. The way in which the Spirit works with us during this journey looks difference from time to time as well as looking different from person to person. In his book *Various Texts on Theology, the Divine Economy, and Virtue and Vice*, St. Maximos writes that "the 'manifestation of the Spirit' (1 Cor. 12:7) is given according to the measure of every man's faith through participation in a particular gift of grace. Thus, every believer is receptive to the energy of the Spirit in a way that corresponds to his degree of faith and the state of his soul; and this energy grants him the capacity needed to carry out a particular commandment."[9]

Our heavenly Father intimately knows and understands us to the point that he is able to work with us depending on the state of our soul at a given time as well as the degree of faith we have at that time. It is in this sense that the workings of the Creator are multifaceted, in that there are many facets or aspects to the movement of the Spirit within our lives and the lives of others around us. St. Maximos elaborates on this concept in another of his books:

> If a man seeks spiritual knowledge, let him plant the foundations of his soul immovably before the Lord, in accordance with God's words to Moses: "Stand here by Me" (Deut. 5:31). But it should be realized that there are differences among those who stand before the Lord, as is clear from the text, "There are some standing here who

---

7. Howard, *Brazos Introduction*, 255.
8. Mulholland, *Invitation to a Journey*, 15.
9. Maximos, *Various Texts*, 186.

will not taste death till they have seen the kingdom of God come with power" (Mark 9:1). For the Lord does not always appear in glory to all who stand before Him. To beginners He appears in the form of a servant (cf. Phil. 2:7); to those able to follow Him as He climbs the high mountain of His transfiguration He appears in the form of God (cf. Matt. 17: 1–9), the form in which He existed before the world came to be (cf. John 17:5). *It is therefore possible for the same Lord not to appear in the same way to all who stand before Him, but to appear to some in one way and to others in another way, according to the measure of each person's faith.*[10]

It must be noted that embracing a multifaceted spiritual formation journey does not mean that there are better or preferred journeys over and above others. Rather it is an acknowledgement that the Creator works with and within each of us individually. "Each of us," St. Maximos writes, "is the steward of his own grace and, if we think logically, we should never envy another person the enjoyment of his gifts, since the disposition which makes us capable of receiving divine blessings depends on ourselves."[11] We are, as St. Paul the Apostle stresses in his letter to the church in Corinth, "all baptized by one Spirit so as to form one body—whether Jews or Gentiles, slave or free—and we were all given the one Spirit to drink. Even so the body is not made up of one part but of many" (1 Corinthians 12:13–14, NIV). Through love and humility, we are to embrace each other's journey with Jesus as we all walk the same path towards the same destination.

Sadly, the multifaceted nature of the workings of the Spirit is commonly missed in modern Christian circles. Writer and pastor Gary Thomas draws attention to this error in his book *Sacred Pathways: Discovering Your Soul's Path to God*. "All too often," he notes, "Christians who desire to be fed spiritually are given the same, generic, hopefully all-inclusive methods . . . Why? Because it's simple, its generic, and it's easy to hold people accountable to.

---

10. Maximos, *Two Hundred Texts*, 140. Emphasis added.
11. Maximos, *Various Texts*, 217–18.

Part 3: The Journey

But, for many Christians, it's just not enough."[12] The answer to this dilemma, according to Thomas, is to embrace the notion that that the different personalities and temperaments given to us by the Creator can be—and should be—reflected in the way in which we worship the Lord.[13] This response harkens back to the multifaceted nature of spiritual formation promoted by St. Maximos.

Rather than trying to force those around us to participate in the same spiritual disciplines that we find valuable, we should advocate a principle of variability in which each person is treated according to their temperament, actions, station in life, and needs. We are to rejoice with each person we meet along the path of life, no matter who they are or how long we walk with them. If the Spirit moves them on ahead or if we are asked to drop back, it is of no consequence for we each are to obey the Lord according to our own journey. In his famous devotional classic *The Imitation of Christ*, Thomas à Kempis (1380–1471) tells us that "not everyone can have the same devotion. One exactly suits this person, another that. Different exercises, likewise, are suitable for different times, some for feast days and some again for weekdays. In time of temptation we need certain devotions. For days of rest and peace we need others. Some are suitable when we are sad, others when we are joyful in the Lord."[14]

In embracing our multifaceted spiritual formation journey, we seek to learn how to discern the dancing hand of the Spirit. The Lord is always at work among us, before us, after us, and through us. In slowing down and embracing the journey, we create space for Jesus to show us what he is doing. This life is not a race to be won or a challenge to be conquered. It is, as Bishop Kallistos Ware notes, "a journey through the inward space of the heart . . . into eternity."[15] Though the type of spiritual exercises we practice may vary from season to season or from person to person, the intentional and ongoing practice of the disciplines will, as M.

---

12. G. Thomas, *Sacred Pathways*, 14.
13. G. Thomas, *Sacred Pathways*, 21.
14. Kempis, *Imitation of Christ*, 19.
15. Ware, *Orthodox Way*, 7.

Robert Mulholland tells us, "becomes a means of grace God works through and moves to transform that dead portion of our body into life in the image of Christ."[16]

Where We Are Going

Over the last few years I have had the pleasure of introducing my oldest son to the joy of backpacking. Our first outing was two-night trip along a 1.5-mile trail to the top of a waterfall in central Idaho on the lands of the Nimiipuu (Nez Perce). The next year, when he was seven, we followed a path deep inside a canyon along the Snake River in the land of Shoshone-Bannock tribes for a few miles before returning to the trailhead to find a fishing hole. The year after that we backpacked five miles into the Sawtooth Wilderness to see yet another waterfall. In hiking with my son, I quickly learned that the destination is an important piece of each journey. Though I was content with just being out in nature, he was focused on what we would do or see once we arrived at our destination. It was the promise of seeing a waterfall or trying to catch a fish that kept him walking forward on the path.

Pentecostal philosopher James K. A. Smith suggests that "we picture human persons not as containers filled with ideas or beliefs, but rather as dynamic, desiring 'arrows' aimed and pointed at something ultimate that in turn becomes a mirror of the sorts of people they (want to) become. We are fundamentally creatures of desire who crave particular visions of the kingdom—the good life—and our desire is shaped and directed by practices that point the heart, as it were."[17] In other words, it is our destination that shapes who we are and how we walk through this life. Accordingly, we must choose our end goal with care as its influence on our journey is beyond measure. As the fifth-century desert father

---

16. Mulholland, *Invitation to a Journey*, 153.
17. Smith, *Desiring the Kingdom*, 71.

Part 3: The Journey

St. Mark the Ascetic so candidly put it, "to journey without direction is wasted effort."[18]

Writing in the eighth or ninth century, St. Hesychios the Priest notes that "a traveler setting out on a long, difficult and arduous journey and foreseeing that he may lose his way when he comes back, will put up signs and guideposts along his path in order to make his return simpler. The watchful man, foreseeing this same thing, will use sacred texts to guide him."[19] Hence it is in opening up the sacred texts of the Scriptures we find our destination for we are not the first to travel along the way of Christ.

In his second letter to the believers in Corinth, St. Paul tells them about the pain and suffering he has endured for telling others about Jesus. Yet despite the "constant danger of death," Paul declares that he will continue to preach the news of Jesus because the "troubles we see will soon be over, but the joys to come will last forever" (2 Corinthians 4:11, 18, TLB). It is the promise of the resurrection that keeps Paul moving forward as he knows death is not the end. In knowing his destination, Paul is able to embrace the journey the Creator has him on despite the pain that comes with walking that path.

Similarly, we are to be an end-time people. Our focus should not be on what physical things we can amass in this life or experiences that we can have. Neither are we to hold out for a reduced view of heaven that includes clouds and harps. Rather we are to join with Jesus in his mission to declare that the kingdom of God has broken into this present evil age. "Our aim," as St. Paul said, "is to please him [Jesus] always, whether we are here in this body or away from this body. For we must all stand before Christ to be judged. We will each receive whatever we deserve for the good or evil we have done in our bodies" (2 Corinthians 5:9–10, TLB).

The great fourth-century desert father St. Antony echoed the words of St. Paul in his encouragement to continue to practice the spiritual disciplines though we may become disheartened:

---

18. Mark, *On the Spiritual Law*, 114.
19. Hesychios, *On Watchfulness and Holiness*, 185.

[L]et us hold in common the same eagerness not to surrender what we have begun, either by growing fainthearted in the labors or by saying, 'We have spent a long time in the discipline.' Rather, as through making a beginning daily, let us increase our dedication . . .

Let us not think that the time is too long or what we do is great, for the sufferings of this present time are not worth comparing with the glory that is to be revealed to us. And let us not consider, when we look at the world, that we have given up things of some greatness, for even the entire earth is itself quite small in relation to all of heaven. If now it happened that we were lords of all the earth, and renounced all the earth, that would amount to nothing as compared with the kingdom of heaven.

For just as if someone might despise one copper drachma in order to gain a hundred gold drachma, so he who is ruler of the whole earth, and renounced it, loses little, and he receives a hundred times more. But if all the earth is not equal in value to the heavens, then he who has given up a few arourae, sacrifices virtually nothing, and even if he should give up a house or considerable wealth, he has no reason to boast or grow careless.

We ought also to realize that if we do not surrender these things through virtue, then later when we die, we shall leave these things behind—often, to those whom we do not wish, as Ecclesiastes reminds us. This being the case, why should we not give them up for virtue's sake, so that we might inherit even a kingdom? Let none among us have even the yearning to possess. For what benefit is there in possessing these things that we do not take with us? Why not rather own those things that we are able to take away with us—such things as prudence, justice, temperance, courage, understanding, love, concern for the poor, faith in Christ, freedom from anger, hospitality? If we possess these, we shall discover them running before, preparing hospitality for us there in the land of the meek.[20]

---

20. Athanasius, *Life of Antony*, 44–46.

Part 3: The Journey

It is focusing on where we are going that enables us to move forward through the ups and downs of life. What we see around us today is not the destination; the destination is the promise of a renewed earth and renewed heaven without any more pain, sorrow, tears, or death (Revelation 21:1–4)—a place in which all our human and nonhuman relatives will live together once again in peace and harmony. It is the desire to see our wonderful Creator and Savior face to face that motivates and transforms us into a people of the Creator. Though our journey along the path of life may look different per the dancing hand of the Spirit, we all have the same destination shaping us. To quote St. Maximos once more, "God is the origin, intermediary state and consummation of all created things . . . for, as Scriptures says, 'All things are from Him and through Him, and have Him as their goal' (Rom. 11:36)."[21] Through his grace and love, we can learn to walk anew along the path of life, one footfall after another.

---

21. Maximos, *Two Hundred Texts*, 116.

— 9 —

Dying in Color

I saw myself dying with a desire to see God, and I knew not how to seek that life otherwise than by dying.

—ST. TERESA OF AVILA[1]

IN THE SPRING OF 2009, I attended a church leadership conference in Galveston, Texas, the home of the now annihilated Karankawa people. Gathering in the Moody Gardens Conference Center, we lifted our voices in worship of the Creator King before listening to a sundry of speakers wax eloquently about the Scriptures, church, leadership, and life. During one of the sessions, Dr. Cherith Fee-Nordling made a comment about how God isn't in the CPR business, but rather he is in the resurrection business.[2] Instead of fighting with God and trying to stay alive, we are to die to ourselves so that he can resurrect us into a new life.

---

1. Teresa, *Life*, 223.
2. Dr. Cherith Fee-Nordling was a guest speaker at the May 2009 Vineyard USA Leadership Conference, entitled "Heroic Leadership in a Time of Change." I do not have a transcript of her talk so I am relying on my memory for this comment. My apologies to Dr. Fee-Nordling if my memory failed me as to the content of her session.

Part 3: The Journey

What made this comment so powerful to me is that nine months earlier I had accepted the position of associate pastor at my local church.[3] Being a pastor was not something I had ever sought out or wanted. The appointment came about through a series of events that required my wife and I to lay aside some of our dreams and hopes. We had to, basically, die to our plans and desires so that God could resurrect us into a new life with new dreams and desires. In writing this over a decade later, I can confirm that the dreams my wife and I had prior to this appointment have stayed dead while the new dreams have continued to flourish. Though we now embrace our current journey, back then it was really, really hard to lay down years of dreaming and planning to walk into the darkness of the unknown.

The Confessor

In his famous poem "Do Not Go Gentle into That Good Night," Welsh poet Dylan Thomas (1914–1953) wrote that "though wise men at their end know dark is right; because their words had forked no lightning they; do not go gentle into that good night."[4] Though written many a moon fall from the time of St. Maximos the Confessor, these words echo the ending of his mortal journey upon this earth. Despite being born into a wealthy aristocratic family in the capital of the Eastern Roman (Byzantine) Empire, St. Maximos laid dying in exile approximately nine hundred miles from the place of his birth and over two thousand miles from the North African town of Carthage, which he called home for many a decade.[5] His body of eighty-two years laid broken, having recently undergone extreme torture at the hands of Emperor Constans II, who supported his theological opponents. To prevent him from preaching or writing, St. Maximos's right hand and tongue were

---

3. The appointment was made in August 2008 at the Payette River Vineyard Christian Fellowship in Sweet, Idaho, under Pastor Brian Harm. The church continues to this day though it is now called Calvary Chapel Sweet.

4. D. Thomas, *Poems*, 239.

5. Louth, *Maximus the Confessor*, 4–5, 16–17.

cut off. Despite this torture, St. Maximos refused to go "gentle into that good night" of death, choosing instead to "rage against the dying of the light"[6] by holding strong to the mystery of the faith while embracing the journey set before him.

Eighteen years after his death, the Sixth Ecumenical Council (680–681) caused lightning to finally fork off the rod of truth held high by St. Maximos when they confirmed his words as true for all of history. Years prior to this, in his *Four Hundred Texts on Love*, St. Maximos wrote that "if you are not indifferent to both fame and dishonor, riches and poverty, pleasure and distress, you have not yet acquired perfect love. For perfect love is indifferent not only to these but even to this fleeting life and to death."[7] St. Maximos lived out these words in that the Way of Christ took him from the riches of Constantinople, where he served as the secretary to Emperor Heraklios, to the poverty of the monastery of Cyzikos and then the deserts of Africa. He went from honor to dishonor, from traveling with bishops and having people rejoice over his words to dying as a condemned man in exile from everyone and everything he loved. It was the perfect love that St. Maximos had for Jesus of Nazareth which carried him forward to the point that we who now journey along the Way know him as the "the Confessor" for his steadfast role in defending the faith against all odds.

Dying to Self

Established in the early fourth century by St. Helena, the mother of Emperor Constantine, the Stavrovouni Monastery in Cyprus in one of the oldest monasteries in the world. Over the entrance into the monastery is a sign of unknown origin that says quite simply, "If you die before you die you shall not die when you die."[8] Though pithy, the saying is quite powerful in that it echoes the words that St. Paul the Apostle wrote to the church in Rome, "If

---

6. D. Thomas, *Poems*, 239.
7. Maximos, *Four Hundred Texts*, 61.
8. Markides, *Gifts of the Desert*, 246.

Part 3: The Journey

you live according to the flesh, you will die; but if by the Spirit you put to death the misdeeds of the body, you will live" (Romans 8:13, NIV). These words, in turn, are but a summarization of Jesus of Nazareth's command to his followers to "deny themselves and take up their cross daily and follow me" (Luke 9:23, NIV). Though the cross has become a mere piece of jewelry to many who live today, the first-century listener in Israel would have seen the cross as a bloody instrument of torture used by the Roman Empire to keep them in line. Hence Jesus' call for them to pick up their cross was an invitation to death.

In reflecting on this call of Jesus, the German theologian and pastor Dietrich Bonhoeffer would write that "when Christ calls a man, he bids him come and die . . . In fact every command of Jesus is a call to die, with all our affections and lusts."[9] Years later British theologian Simon Ponsonby would echo this sentiment when he declared that those who "desire more of God will constantly learn the painful lesson of personal crucifixion. Only as we die do we live, only as we lay down our lives are they resurrected in the power of the Spirit, only as we hide ourselves in the wounds of Christ is the ongoing healing, saving power of the cross manifested through us."[10]

To know Jesus, then, is to embrace the pain of dying. We must let go of our dreams, passions, plans, and goals. It does not matter if these dreams and goals are worthy or unworthy, holy or unholy—the fact remains that to follow the man from Nazareth we must let go of ourselves and allow him to remake us into his image. As St. Maximos once commented, "the man of intelligence will choose to die voluntarily according to the flesh before the advent of that death which comes whether he likes it or not."[11] This, dare I say, is just as hard in modern America as it was in first-century Israel. No matter our culture, we all seek to preserve our life rather than letting go. "Self," as writer Carl Medearis reminds us, "is no longer the most important commodity. Living in the wisdom and

---

9. Bonhoeffer, *Cost of Discipleship*, 89–90.
10. Ponsonby, *More*, 182–83.
11. Maximos, *Various Texts*, 254.

compassion of the true Way, the life of the Nazarene, is in itself a death of sorts. It is a daily ritual of surrender to the here and now of self-interest. In order to live like this, we must model ourselves after the Christ, pursuing relationships, compassion, and even reckless self-endangerment as a sacrifice to this person, this Way. Jesus' way embraces this cost as a means of living in the pleasure of the kingdom of heaven."[12]

Colors of Death

Five hundred years before St. Maximos, another starwort defender of the faith would set out on a journey that would ultimately lead to death. The gentleman in question is none other than St. Ignatius, the third bishop of Antioch after St. Peter the apostle. During the reign of Emperor Trajan (98–117) St. Ignatius was arrested on account of his allegiance to Jesus and taken to Rome "through Asia under the strictest military surveillance."[13] Along the way, St. Ignatius wrote seven letters of encouragement to the various church communities he passed through. His letter to the church in Rome stands out as he looks forward to his coming martyrdom with enthusiasm while telling the Roman Christians not to prevent it.[14] Though this sentiment may sound strange to our modern ears, for St. Ignatius martyrdom was just another way he could imitate the Lord Jesus Christ. "When there is no trace of my body left for the world to see," St. Ignatius wrote, "then I shall truly be Jesus Christ's disciple."[15]

Martyrdom is not a subject normally talked about in churches of the United States for we have become complacent with wealth, comfort, and power. If we do talk about it, it is usually in context of the cultural wars, where someone is claiming to be a martyr because they were asked to do something they disagreed with. It was not always this way as the journey of St. Ignatius shows. In the

---

12. Medearis, *Speaking of Jesus*, 156.
13. Eusebius, *Church History*, 167.
14. Staniforth and Louth, trans., *Apostolic Fathers*, 56.
15. Ignatius, *Epistle to the Romans*, 86.

early days of the church, martyrdom was a normal part of the faith. As scholar Alfred Rush notes, to be a martyr was to be both a "witness and sufferer, a witness to the truth and a sufferer for Christ."[16] In his book *Water from a Deep Well*, Gerald Sittser, a professor of theology at Whitworth University in Spokane, Washington, states that "martyrdom is foundational to our understanding Christian spirituality, for it highlights what was—and still is—distinctive and essential in Christianity."[17] Namely that the followers of Jesus have a choice between "Christ and something else that vies for our ultimate allegiance."[18]

While not all Christians will be asked to physically die for their adherence to the Way of Life, we will all be asked at some point—and probably multiple times—to choose which path we will take. In recognition of this, the historical church came to distinguish three different degrees of martyrdom:

> Pope Gregory I, in his *Homilia in Evangelia*, explains three modes of martyrdom, designated by the colors red, blue (or green), and white. This triad is unique but draws on earlier distinctions between 'red' and 'white' martyrdom. 'Red' martyrdom involved violent death as a result of religious persecution. Saint Jerome had used the term 'white martyrdom' for those such as desert hermits who aspired to the conditions of martyrdom through strict asceticism. The distinction is marked by Gregory between inward and outward martyrdom. Blue (or green) martyrdom involved the denial of desires, as through fasting and penitent labors, without necessarily implying a journey or complete withdrawal from life, while red martyrdom requires torture or death.[19]

---

16. Rush, "Spiritual Martyrdom."
17. Sittser, *Water from a Deep Well*, 47.
18. Sittser, *Water from a Deep Well*, 47–48.
19. Driscoll and Joncas, *Order of Mass*, 95.

Dying in Color

Red Martyrdom

St. Stephen was the first to follow the Way of Jesus in death when the crowds of Jerusalem stoned him (Acts 7:57–60). A few years later St. James the brother of John was killed at the order of King Herod Agrippa for daring to follow the Risen King (Acts 12:1–2). Countless other followers of the Way would lay down their lives over the following years. Some would even die gruesome deaths in the Roman theaters of the day as entertainment for the common citizen and a warning for those who considered converting to Christianity. The violent persecution of the followers of Jesus by the evil one failed in that the spectators were astonished at the courage and commitment of the red martyrs.

It is their commitment to Jesus in which lies the greatest value of these martyrs. No matter how violent the enemy was, they remained steadfast in their passionate love for Jesus. Though he technically escape the red martyrdom, St. Maximos embraced the path and stood firm on the truths of Jesus despite experiencing multiple torture sessions designed to force him to relent. As St. Polycarp declared when asked to deny Jesus, "Eighty and six years I have served Him, and He has done me no wrong. How then can I blaspheme my King and Savior?"[20] Though we in the United States may never have to pay the ultimate price for following Jesus, we can learn from their unwavering belief that Jesus' lordship over our lives challenges all other claims—wealth, status, power, and nationalism.[21] Jesus alone is King and there is no other.

White Martyrdom

A seventh- or early-eighth-century Irish homily describes the white martyrs as those who "part for the sake of God from everything that they love, although they may suffer fasting and hard work thereby."[22] The desert fathers of the fourth and fifth centuries

---

20. Evarestus, *Martyrdom of Polycarp*, 128.
21. Sittser, *Water from a Deep Well*, 28.
22. Davies, ed., *Celtic Spirituality*, 370.

Part 3: The Journey

are the most well-known martyrs of this color. St. Maximos himself embraced the white martyrdom when he left behind the wealth of his family and pledged himself to the monastic life.[23] Seeking to follow Jesus with all their heart, soul, strength, and mind (Luke 10:27), the white martyrs gave up fleshly comforts (e.g., soft beds, nice clothes, conveniences, regular meals, etc.) and embraced a life of simplicity and self-sacrifice. As Alfred Rush notes, "in contrast to actual martyrdom [red martyrdom], where external bodily death takes place, spiritual martyrdom [white martyrdom] is interior. It is an affair of the heart, of the soul. It is the hidden asceticism of the practice of virtue and the overcoming of vice, a process in which the person overcomes not the pagan tyrant but the tyranny within himself."[24]

The thought of giving away one's material possessions to pursue Jesus may sound strange and extreme to most twenty-first-century Christians in the United States of America. Capitalism and materialism have so enveloped American culture that such thoughts of simplicity and self-sacrifice are rarely, if ever, heard or contemplated. The desert fathers, however, beckon the believer of today to resist the seductive nature of modern culture and fight the battle raging within our own hearts.[25] Hence the white martyrdom is about recognizing the forces at work that cause a person to desire something they currently do not have while simultaneously embracing an indifferent attitude towards material items. Rather than pursuing riches and the American dream, modern Jesus followers would do better to promote economic equality and sustainability while living simply and generously.

Rick Williams in his short book *Uncomfortable Growth* makes note that "one of the subtle religious appeals of consumerism is that it offers a new immediacy, a living alternative to God's reality and what is still to come. By being offered 'heaven now', people give up the ultimate quest in pursuit of that which can be immediately

---

23. Louth, *Maximus the Confessor*, 5.
24. Rush, "Spiritual Martyrdom," 574.
25. Sittser, *Water from a Deep Well*, 94.

Dying in Color

consumed."[26] The lives and actions of the white martyrs, both past and present, provide us with an alternative to this siren call. In embracing the concepts of simplicity and self-sacrifice modeled by these martyrs, the modern Christian enters into a place that allows them to see how damaging modern culture is to the spiritual life.[27] As they continue to walk down the self-sacrificial path of the white martyrs, their soul will find rest and they will, like the fathers of old, be able to demonstrate the love of Jesus to the world around them in practical ways.

Green Martyrdom

The final color of death is that of the green martyrs. The origins of this martyrdom hearken back to the late fifth and early sixth centuries in Ireland.[28] Lacking the violent social pressures that gave rise to the red martyrs, the monks of the green isle followed the example of the white martyrs in fighting the forces of virtue and vice within their own hearts.[29] However, rather than building monasteries in hard-to-reach places, the green martyrs of Ireland deliberately built their communities in locations accessible to the people at large.[30] This allowed them to expand their reach and to preach the good news of Jesus to everyone on the island.

The path of the green martyr is therefore a path of spiritual martyrdom combined with active evangelism and service to those around them. This is a hard road for the siren calls of consumerism and society pressures are strong. We all want to fit in and to belong. To embrace the color green is to daily fight against such pressures while actively putting oneself in the position to be overwhelmed. This is why the green martyrs placed such a high value on community, for it is only in community with each other that they were

---

26. R. Williams, *Uncomfortable Growth*, 114–15.
27. Sittser, *Water from a Deep Well*, 93.
28. Cahill, *How the Irish Saved*, 131.
29. Rush, "Spiritual Martyrdom," 574.
30. Hunter, *Celtic Way of Evangelism*, 28.

able to continue walking the path of spiritual martyrdom while surrounded by the waters of this world.

Embracing Death

Three colors of death: red, white, and green. Though we all are called to die to ourselves, the Wind of the Lord may ask some of us to embrace one or more of these colors. To walk into the darkness of the unknown is to trust the Creator while knowing where we are going. It is not just the persecution that comes from the outside, but also the struggle within our hearts and souls—the wrestling that we do with our pride and flesh as we seek to obey and live out the commandments of Jesus. These commandments are often in direct conflict with our own personal interests and desires. Whether bitter or sweet, each situation is a gift from God, molding and shaping us to be his people. "He who like Job and the courageous martyrs," St. Maximos wrote in encouragement, "bears the assaults of unsought-for trials and temptations with an unshakeable will is a powerful lamp: for by his bravery and patience he keeps the light of salvation burning, since he possesses the Lord as his strength and his song (cf Ps. 1 18:14)."[31]

If we are called to die in color, then may we do so with courage and faith with the name of our Lord on our lips. And even if we do not embrace the red, white, and green of death, may we learn from these martyrs and put into practice the lessons they teach us. In his classic book *Beginning to Pray*, Metropolitan Anthony Bloom reminds us that each day is blessed by God no matter what happens within those twenty-four-hours:

> This day is blessed by God, it is God's own and now let us go into it. You walk in this day as God's own messenger; whomever you meet, you meet in God's own way. You are there to be the presence of the Lord God, the presence of Christ, the presence of the Spirit, the presence of the Gospel—this is your function on this particular day. God has never said that when you walk into a situation in

---

31. Maximos, *Various Texts*, 255.

Dying in Color

His own Name, He will be crucified, and you will be the risen one. You must be prepared to walk into situations, one after the other, in God's name, to walk as the Son of God had done: in humiliation and humility, in truth and ready to be persecuted and so forth. Usually what we expect when we fulfill God's commandment is to see a marvelous result at once—we read of that at times in the lives of the saints. When, for instance, someone hits us on one cheek, we turn the other one, although we don't expect to be hit at all, but we expect to hear the other person say 'What, such humility'—you get your reward and he gets the salvation of his soul.

It does not work that way. You must pay the cost and very often you get hit hard. What matters is that you are prepared for that. As to the day, if you accept that this day was blessed of God, chosen by God with His own hand, then every person you meet is a gift of God, every circumstance you will meet is a gift of God, whether it is bitter or sweet, whether you like it or dislike it. It is God's own gift to you and if you take it that way, then you can face any situation. But then you must face it with the readiness that anything may happen, whether you enjoy it or not, and if you walk in the name of the Lord through a day which has come fresh and new out of His own Hands and has been blessed for you to live with it, then you can make prayer and life really like the two sides of one coin. You act and pray in one breath, as it were, because all the situations that follow one another require God's blessing.[32]

---

32. Bloom, *Beginning to Pray*, 76–77.

— 10 —

Chasing the Wild Goose

*The only stuff that happens, happens along the way.
Get going and see what happens.*

—KEN WILSON[1]

*Many are the plans in a person's heart,
but it is the Lord's purpose that prevails.*

—SOLOMON, SON OF DAVID, KING OF ISRAEL[2]

THERE WAS A WAR going on inside of me. A few months earlier my wife and I had joined a church-planting team with the goal of helping start a new multisite location in a small rural community about forty miles north of Boise, Idaho, on the traditional lands of the Shoshone-Bannock people. We had joined the team at the request of our pastor, who needed some warm bodies to help with the miscellaneous tasks that go along with starting a new church. After praying about it, we agreed drive up to the community once

---

1. Wilson, *Jesus Brand Spirituality*, 66.
2. Proverbs 19:21, NIV.

a week for six months to help with the children's ministry while the new congregation was formed.[3]

Three months into our commitment the members of the church asked my wife and me to move to the community and join the church permanently. This, as you can imagine, was a huge request, as we had no desire to move from the big city to a small rural community with one gas station, a bar, and a restaurant. Less than two years previously we had bought our first house and were enjoying living within a few miles of our work, in-laws, and main church campus. Saying yes to the new church's request would mean a major life change as well as a large financial loss, since my wife was not willing to commute back and forth from the new community to the large city for work.

Not knowing what to do, I attended a Saturday morning men's prayer and healing breakfast at the main campus. While I did not personally need any physical healing, I was hoping that I could siphon off a bit of God's presence and receive an answer to my dilemma. Halfway through the meeting I felt a strong urge to take a motorcycle ride up to the community where we were being asked to move. In moment of stupidity, I found myself arguing with Spirit as I had paid ten dollars to attend the prayer breakfast and I felt that I had to stay to get my money's worth. Luckily, I soon came to my senses and obeyed the voice of the Lord to leave the meeting and go on a morning ride into the mountains.

Arriving in the community, I saw a garage sale sign that seemed to stand out to me. Pulling over, I looked over the various items before engaging in conversation with the couple hosting the sale. As it turned out, they had recently started attending the new church and had questions about it. A few moments later another couple pulled up to look over the items for sale. Since we were talking about the new church, it was easy to ask the new folks if they wanted to attend the service the following day. They were open

---

3. The multisite church started in the early months of 2006 with the first service being held in the evening of March 19 in Sweet, Idaho. Tri Robinson of the Vineyard Boise Christian Fellowship (Boise, Idaho) was the founding pastor of both the congregations and the one who invited my wife and me to join the church planting team.

to the concept and eventually became followers of Jesus and solid members of the church for years come.

After a bit more chit chatting, I climbed onto my motorcycle and drove north through the community. At the other end of the valley there was a second garage sale, so I pulled over. This sale was being hosted by a lady who was helping move her mother out of the community. In talking to her, I soon found that she was a recovering drug addict who attended a twelve-step program at our church's main campus. I also discovered that her mom's move was not planned, but rather was an eviction. As I prayed for her and her mother, it seemed that the Wind of the Living God was directing the day and showing me the needs of the community.

Driving north once again, I left the collection of houses and continued onward for another fifteen or so miles until I came upon another small community tucked into the central mountains of Idaho. As I drove through the town, tears began to fall down my face and cloud my vision. Pulling over on a small rise, I removed my helmet and looked down over the town. In my heart, I heard the Lord ask, "Who will tell these people about me?" In the years prior to this trip, I had the privilege of traveling to various other countries on short-term mission trips. I had even hiked into the jungles of the Philippines to deliver medical supplies to small villages of less than five hundred souls. And here I was, looking over a community of maybe one hundred people while thinking about moving to its larger neighbor of maybe two hundred souls. I had gladly traveled the world to tell people about Jesus, but would I give up my nice house, easy commute, and big-city lifestyle to tell these people about Jesus? That was the question that now burned inside my heart.

The Legend

Popular legend states that the Celtic believers of the British Isles used the wild goose to symbolize the Holy Spirit instead of the traditional dove. Unlike the dove, which is calm and gentle, a wild goose will attack you and is untamed and uncontrollable. In similar fashion, the Breath of God is unpredictable, moving like the wind and disturbing the status quo where he goes (John 3:8). When combined with the more modern phrase "wild goose chase," the symbolism of the wild goose becomes a recipe for mystery and adventure. To chase a wild goose is to embark on something foolish or hopeless. Yet if the Holy Spirit is the Wild Goose, then everything changes. Things that seem foolish to us become wise in the sight of the Almighty as we trade worldly security for radical obedience, judgment for mercy, and our life for his life.

Though the symbolism of the Wild Goose most likely arose from the Iona Community in the early twentieth-century and not from the early Celtic believers as commonly stated, I believe there is something wonderful about the concept.[4] Throughout the Scriptures there are multiple symbols used to describe the Holy Spirit with the most famous symbols being the dove, fire, oil, water, and wind. In each instance the writers of Scripture tried to capture a part of the indescribable mystery of the Spirit of the Creator. Our culture today is in need a new symbol of the Spirit to catch our imaginations. The symbol of the Wild Goose is one that beckons us to follow Jesus into the great mystery of the unknown. It is a wild, mysterious symbol that challenges us to go beyond our daily life.

On that day when I was parked on the side of the road crying, I remember looking up and seeing a wild goose flying over that small community. I don't know if it was a real-life Canada goose or if it was just a vision of a goose. Either way, seeing a lone goose flying over the fields and houses that day broke my heart. Going back home, I told my wife about the legend of the Wild Goose and what I had experience that day. Together we made the decision to throw caution to the wind and follow the Wild Goose on a new adventure into the unknown of the future.

---

4. Bradley, *Celtic Christianity*, 211.

Part 3: The Journey

Life on the Edge

Fifteen years have gone by since my wife and I decided to follow the Wild Goose. Though we have continued to try to live with hands wide open, ready for the Wind to direct us, we have spent most of that time working and raising a family. It may sound crazy, but for us, two young people with a heart for the nations, staying home in the United States and helping start a new church was life on the edge. We even turned down a request from a church in Chile, South America, to join their work. It seemed like the Wild Goose wasn't done with us in Idaho.

Eventually, as I noted in the previous chapter, the church asked me to be their associate pastor and then senior pastor. Every day for nine years I woke up, got dressed, and drove an hour to my work as a brand-protection analyst before embarking on another hour drive back home. Evenings and weekends were spent helping with the church, talking to people, preparing sermons, and the like. It wasn't a very glamorous life or one that would make the front page of a missionary or church journal. It was just life.

Here's the point: following the Wild Goose means doing different things depending on what God wants you to do. It is being willing to say yes to the Wild Goose when you want to say no. Some of you who are reading this book may follow the dancing hand of the Spirit into talking to your next-door neighbor, church planting, international missions, volunteering at a local food pantry, homeless ministry, small-group hosting, or, perhaps, to a new job. Each of these paths are legitimate paths into the darkness of the unknown. For those who follow Jesus, writer Calvin Miller notes, "the world becomes a 'going' place rather than a residing place."[5] We are to go into all the world and preach the good news of the Jesus Christ to all of creation (Mark 16:15).

In his book *The Hobbit*, fantasy writer and Jesus follower J. R. R. Tolkien describes the awakening of a very respectable hobbit, Bilbo Baggins, who came from a long line of respectable hobbits. The Bagginses were respectable not only because they were

---

5. Miller, *Path of Celtic Prayer*, 78.

rich, but because "they never had any adventures or did anything unexpected."[6] Then one day a wizard and thirteen dwarves showed up unannounced at Biblo's door. Being a kind and hospitable hobbit, Bilbo invited them in for tea though he really didn't need the bother. After the meal, the dwarves began to sing and as they sang "something Tookish woke up inside him, and he wished to go and see the great mountains, and hear the pine-trees and the waterfalls, and explore the caves, and wear a sword instead of a walking-stick."[7]

Chasing the Wild Goose means be willing to do something you don't want to do—like host a party of dwarves—because it seemed like the thing to do at that moment. And when we do that—when we step out beyond our comfort zones—we find the Wild Goose waiting for us and beckoning us to follow him. "Faith," Calvin Miller tells us, "is never a resting place. As soon as new disciples enter the fortress of faith, they find they must leave again. They willingly take up the dangerous life of a world-changer. Change has come to them personally along with a command to effect in the world what they have lately experienced. Bringing more change."[8] Each of us who have chosen to follow the path of the Way with our Lord and Savior, Jesus of Nazareth, must be willing to live on the edge.

An Intertwined Trinity (Revisited)

At the onset of this book I stated that our goal was to look at how embracing an open-handed view of the mystery of the faith opens the door to a way of life in which each person's journey is different. St. Maximos the Confessor has been our guide throughout this conversation with his words illuminating our path and providing signposts pointing us forward. His theology, which is based upon the mystery of the incarnation, propels us into a way of life

---

6. Tolkien, *Hobbit*, 4.
7. Tolkien, *Hobbit*, 19.
8. Miller, *Path of Celtic Prayer*, 77–78.

Part 3: The Journey

centered on loving Jesus. This love, in turn, directs us outward toward our fellow sisters and brothers with a realization that each of us journeys along the path of Christ differently.

Though it is tempting to separate these three concepts, they actually need each other to fully blossom. The Mystery of the faith needs the movement and love of the Way, for without it we would fall into agnosticism, where nothing is certain. The inaugurated atonement of the Way needs the Mystery to keep it from being yet another system of dogmatic points and beliefs. The Way also needs the spiritual formation of the Journey to remind us of the destination toward which we travel. Similarly, the multifaceted nature of the Journey needs the Mystery and the Way to help people understand that we are all in the process of being transformed into the image of our Beloved.

Unspoken yet buried deep within all three of these concepts is the virtue of humility, for without it we cannot even begin to embrace the Mystery, the Way, and the Journey. Clinical psychologist Robert J. Wicks reflects on the value of the church mothers and fathers when he defines humility as the "ability to fully appreciate our innate gifts and our current 'growing edges' in ways that enable us to learn, act, and flow with our lives as never before."[9] Being humble is about being open-handed with one's journey and thoughts, knowing that we are constantly growing and changing. Doing this, Wicks notes, opens our lives up for simplicity, gratefulness, honesty, generosity, transparency, and forgiveness as well as "space for doubt and deeper questions rather than filling ourselves with false certainty and pat answers."[10] This sentiment echoes that of St. Maximos as seen within his book *Four Hundred Texts on Love*:

> The person who fears the Lord has humility as his constant companion and, through the thoughts which humility inspires, reaches a state of divine love and thankfulness. For he recalls his former worldly way of life, the various sins he has committed and the temptations which has befallen him since youth; and he recalls,

---

9. Wicks, *Inner Life*, 8.
10. Wicks, *Inner Life*, 10–11.

too, how the Lord delivered him from all this, and how he led him away from a passion-dominated life to a life ruled by God. Then, together with fear, he also receives love, and in deep humility continually gives thanks to the Benefactor and Helmsman of our lives.[11]

Humility drives us back to the Creator in that it seeks to remind us of our "growing edges" and previous missteps. Embracing humility as a constant companion means we are putting to death the pride within ourselves and allowing the Spirit of Life to surge through us, propelling us forward with Jesus in thanksgiving and love.

Go Gaily in the Dark

In G. K. Chesterton's epic poem *The Ballad of the White Horse* there is a stanza that reads, "The men of the East may spell the stars, And times and triumphs mark, But the men signed of the cross of Christ, Go gaily in the dark."[12] For Chesterton, the "men of the East" are those who do not know Jesus as their King. For these men, the darkness of the unknown fills them with fear so they try hard to predict what will happen. The followers of Jesus, however, do not follow this path. "Predicting the future," as American scholar and writer Thomas Cahill mentions, "is an occupation for pagans, not Christians."[13] Instead we "go gaily in the dark," walking hand in hand with our Beloved Jesus.

Walking into the darkness of the unknown is scary for we know not what will happen. We do not know if we will be asked to embrace the colors of death or if the Wild Goose will lead us across the street in our own neighborhood. The only thing we know for sure is that Jesus has marked us with the Holy Spirit (Ephesians 1:13) and promised to go with us into the darkness (Matthew 28:20). "Real faith has room for doubt," pastor Brian Zahnd tells us, "understanding that the effort to believe is the very thing that

---

11. Maximos, *Four Hundred Texts*, 56.
12. Chesterton, *Ballad of the White Horse*.
13. Cahill, *Mysteries of the Middle Ages*, 178.

Part 3: The Journey

makes doubt possible. Real faith is not afraid of doubt, but the faux faith of certitude is afraid of its own shadow."[14] In spite of our doubt, we walk forward into the darkness of the unknown holding the hand of our Beloved, for he is trustworthy.

The focus of this text has been on three beautifully intertwined concepts that have the potential to lead us forward through the messiness of life. Though the culture around us—both within and without Christianity—swirls in confusion of rote answers to complex questions, we can embrace an open-handed view of the faith, knowing that we have but barely seen the fullness of God. Holding in humility what we know about the Creator allows us to embrace a movement-centric view of salvation as seen through the concept of an inaugurated atonement way of life. Coupled together, the Mystery and the Way give birth to a multifaceted spiritual formation Journey where Jesus reveals himself to each person according to their needs.

Permeating throughout the intertwined concepts of the Mystery, the Way, and the Journey is another trinity of sorts: love, faith, and hope. First described by St. Paul the Apostle in his epistle to the church in Corinth (1 Corinthians 13:13), these three theological virtues provide the glue that keeps us walking in the way of our Savior along the path of the Mystery, the Way, and the Journey. It is our love for Jesus that starts our journey and keeps us moving forward with him while faith allows us to trust him as we embark into the darkness of life. Hope provides the destination toward which we walk, knowing that we do not have to "rage against the dying of the light"[15] like Dylan Thomas wrote but rather we can "go gaily in the dark"[16] like G. K. Chesterton said with our Lover at our side. Returning to St. Maximos the Confessor one last time, he summarizes the theological virtues in a manner that points us forward into the darkness of the unknown along the path of the Mystery, the Way, and the Journey:

---

14. Zahnd, *Water to Wine*, 231.
15. D. Thomas, *Poems*, 239.
16. Chesterton, *Ballad of the White Horse*.

> Love is the consummation of all blessings, since all who walk in it love leads and guides towards God, the supreme blessing and cause of every blessing, and unites them with Him; for love is faithful and never fails (cf.1 Cor. 13:8). Faith is the foundation of what comes after it, namely hope and love, since it provides a firm basis for truth. Hope is the strength of the two pre-eminent gifts of love and faith, since hope gives us glimpses both of that in which we believe and of that for which we long, and teaches us to make our way towards our goal. Love is the completion of the other two, embracing entirely the entire desire of all desires, and satisfying the yearning of our faith and hope for it; for that which we believe to be and which we hope will come to pass, love enables us to enjoy as a present reality.[17]

At the onset on this text I mentioned that embracing a concept is akin to embracing a human in that both take trust. When we lean in to hug someone, we have to trust that they will not hurt us. Embracing people we know is easier than embracing those we don't know as they have a track record of trust behind them. In between those ends are those people whom we don't know but who have been recommended to us by those we trust. It is my prayer that the concepts of the Mystery, the Way, and the Journey fall into this category. Within these pages I have tried to introduce you to these three beautifully intertwined concepts in hopes that you will find joy and hope within them as I have. In closing, allow me to pray a journeying prayer over you as you walk into the darkness of the unknown.

> **"A Journeying Prayer"**
> **by Andy Freeman and Pete Greig**[18]
> Jesus, take me once again on a journey.
> Take me to the city,
> Take me to the valley and to the mountain,
> Take me to the desert.
> Take me to the place of wandering,

---

17. Maximos, *Various Texts*, 170.
18. Freeman and Greig, *Punk Monk*, 180.

Part 3: The Journey

The place of hunger,
The place of solitude and of pain.
Take me to the place where You seem so far away
Yet only You are there.
Remove my crutches of possessions,
Remove the pillars of my faithless life,
Remove all the thumbs I suck.
And there in that place where nothing is left,
There refine my soul.
Amen.

Acknowledgements

I don't recall very many meals. In fact, I don't really know what I had for breakfast this morning beyond the stereotypical cereal answer. However, there is one meal I remember, and it wasn't due to the quality of the food. Rather it is what happened at that meal that marks it in my heart. It was lunchtime on Friday, July 4, 2008, and my wife and I were at a hotel restaurant near Los Angeles International Airport (LAX). We were traveling with another couple from our home church in Boise, Idaho, to Chile and Paraguay, South America. While en route, we stepped out of the airport to have lunch with some friends of our travel companions who lived in the Los Angeles area. Though I wouldn't know it for many years, the group's decision to eat lunch at that particular hotel ended up changing my life and shifting my perspective on the world.

So, what happened at that fateful lunch oh so many years ago? As only the Divine can coordinate, there was an Eastern Orthodox Church conference happening at that hotel on that day.[1] A few tables over from where we sat were a few priests chatting away over lunch while wearing their trademark black cassocks. Being a tad bored with the table conversation in front of me, I decided to walk over and see if I could start a conversation with the priests. After a short chat, one of the priests led me out of the restaurant to the resource table in the adjoining conference room. Picking up

---

1. It was the 2008 Diocesan Parish Life Conference hosted by St. Nicholas Antiochian Orthodox Christian Cathedral in the Los Angeles Airport Marriott on July 2–6, 2008.

Acknowledgements

five books about the Eastern Orthodox faith, he gave them to me free of charge. As I read those books, my eyes were opened, and my heart was warmed. Though I didn't agree with everything in those books, they did introduce me to the mystery of the faith. For the first time, I had words to explain the Wild Goose chase I was on. And for that reason, this book is dedicated to that anonymous priest who took the time to chat with a stranger and left him with some books.

In the language of my people, the Tsalagi (Cherokee), "Thank you" is "*Wado*." Accordingly, I would like to offer up a huge *wado* to my wonderful bride and fellow sojourner, Emily. Without your encouragement and support I would not be the person I am today. Words can never express the love and gratitude I feel towards you. I am proud to be your love and to the one you chose to run into the darkness of the unknown with. May we never stop chasing the Wild Goose! And to my three sons, *wado* for giving me the space to write. I know it was hard waiting for me to finish before getting to play. Hopefully one day you will read these words and be blessed.

I would like to thank the professors and faculty of St. Stephen's University (SSU) in St. Stephen, New Brunswick, Canada. Under the guidance of Dr. Peter Fitch, SSU's program introduced me to the desert fathers, St. John of the Cross, St. Therese of Lisieux, and other mothers and fathers of the faith. Though joining this program was a step into the darkness for me, it has become a lifesaver in so many ways. As such, I want to say thank you to Dr. Peter Fitch, Dr. Walter Thiessen, Dr. Brad Jersak, and Lorna Jones for allowing me to join your classes and pester you all with questions. It has been a wonderful journey. As this book is based primarily upon my MA thesis, I would like to thank Dr. Brad Jersak for guiding me through the thesis process and Dr. Ron Dart for being the second reader. A huge thanks also to the SSU and St. Croix Church community for your hospitality and welcoming spirit. You all made the trip out from Idaho a blessed time.

Wado also to the Vineyard Boise's VinArts Writers Group: Travis and Kathy Nelson, Dana Long, and April McHugh. Your

Acknowledgements

monthly feedback, encouragement, and support throughout the writing process was invaluable! And may your names be in print under a title one day soon!

Last but not least, I would like to express my gratitude towards Cari Bickel, who patiently and diligently reviewed not only this manuscript, but also my thesis and all the other grad school papers. Your friendship and editing skills are without comparison!! May the Creator continue to pour out his spirit and blessings upon you while your feet find solid ground to walk upon. *Wado* also to the early readers of this manuscript as your feedback was invaluable: Vickie J. S. Hieb, Tura Zapata, Dave Washburn, and Bill Miller. May you all always find a good book to read.

There is no word for "goodbye" among the Tsalagi. Rather we just say "*Donadagohvi*" ("Until we met again").

About the Author

JOSHUA IS A PASSIONATE follower of the Creator King with a missional heart and a love of people. He considers himself a Christian mystic with an emphasis on living out the inaugurated eschatology of kingdom theology within one's daily life. By holding in tension the victory and suffering of the cross, Joshua seeks to embrace the missional journey of following Jesus while knowing that he is saved, being saved, and will one day be saved. Furthermore, he holds to a centered-set mindset that focuses on the personal journey of individual people rather than a one-time event established through doctrine, theology, or tradition.

Joshua is a citizen of the Cherokee Nation of Celtic-Cherokee heritage who grew up in the foothills of the Oklahoma Ozarks on the land of the Cherokees and Osage people, as well as in the pine forests of Northeast Texas on the traditional lands of the Caddo Nation, before moving west to the high mountain desert lands of the Shoshone-Bannock people in Idaho. Married for over twenty years, he and his wife, Emily, have had the privilege of sharing the love of God with people across three continents and nine countries. In 2006 they moved to Sweet, Idaho, a small rural village in the traditional lands of the Shoshone and Bannock people, where they helped start and then led the Sweet Vineyard Christian Fellowship (formerly known as the Payette River Vineyard). They turned the leadership of the church over to a new couple in June 2014 and embarked on a fresh adventure with the Creator King. In October 2018, they moved to Kuna, Idaho, with the goal of

About the Author

creating a faith community focused on helping people explore the mystery of the Creator.

Joshua is the author of *The Here and Not Yet: What Is Kingdom Theology and Why Does It Matter?* (Vineyard International, 2017) as well as an avid blogger at WildGooseChase.org. Joshua holds a BS in business administration and minor in cross-cultural studies from LeTourneau University (Longview, Texas) along with an MA in theology and culture through St. Stephen's University (St. Stephen, New Brunswick, Canada). He has also been awarded a certificate of ministry through Vineyard Leadership Institute (VLI).

Bibliography

Anselm of Canterbury. *Proslogion*. In *The Prayers and Meditations of Saint Anselm*, translated by Benedicta Ward, 238–47. Harmondsworth, England: Penguin, 1986.
Athanasius. *The Life of Antony and the Letter to Marcellinus*. Translated by Robert C. Gregg. Mahwah, NJ: Paulist, 1980.
Bates, Matthew W. *Salvation by Allegiance Alone: Rethinking Faith, Works and the Gospel of Jesus the King*. Grand Rapids: Baker Academic, 2017.
Bernard of Clairvaux. *Bernard of Clairvaux: Selected Works*. Translated by G. R. Evans. New York: Paulist, 1987.
Blin-Bolt, Marie-Dominique. "Darkness as a Metaphor for God in the Work of St. John of the Cross." Master's thesis, Westminster Theological Centre, 2017.
Bloom, Anthony. *Beginning to Pray*. Mahwah, NJ: Paulist, 1970.
Bonhoeffer, Dietrich. *The Cost of Discipleship*. New York: Touchstone, 1995.
Boyd, Gregory A. *God at War: The Bible and Spiritual Conflict*. Downers Grove, IL: InterVarsity, 1997.
———. *The Myth of a Christian Nation: How the Quest for Political Power Is Destroying the Church*. Grand Rapids: Zondervan, 2005.
Bradley, Ian. *Celtic Christianity: Making Myths and Chasing Dreams*. New York: St. Martin's, 1999.
Cahill, Thomas. *How the Irish Saved Civilization: The Untold Story of Ireland's Heroic Role from the Fall of Rome to the Rise of Medieval Europe*. New York: Nan A. Talese, 1995.
———. *Mysteries of the Middle Ages: And the Beginning of the Modern World*. New York: Nan A. Talese, 2008.
Carroll, Lewis. *Alice's Adventures in Wonderland*. Boston: International Pocket Library, 1941.
Chaput, Charles. "Remembering Who We Are and the Story We Belong To." Speech delivered at the Bishops' Symposium, Notre Dame, Indiana, October 19, 2016. *National Catholic Register*. http://www.ncregister.com/daily-news/remembering-who-we-are-and-the-story-we-belong-to.
Chaucer, Geoffrey. *The Parlament of Foules*. Edited by Thomas Raynesford Lounsbury. Boston: Ginn, Heath, 1883.

Bibliography

Chesterton, G. K. *The Ballad of the White Horse.* Ebook. Project Gutenberg, 2013. https://www.gutenberg.org/files/1719/1719-h/1719-h.htm.

Clément, Olivier. *The Roots of Christian Mysticism: Texts from the Patristic Era with Commentary.* 2nd ed. Hyde Park, NY: New City, 2017.

Coniaris, Anthony M. *Introducing the Orthodox Church: Its Faith and Life.* Minneapolis: Light and Life, 1982.

Conniry, Charles J,. Jr. "The Western World's Loss and (Partial) Recover of Mystery." *The Journal of NAIITS: An Indigenous Learning Community* 12 (2014) 27–43.

Dart, Ron. "Certainty, Uncertainty and Wisdom: The Christian Tradition." *Clarion Journal*, August 28, 2020. https://www.clarion-journal.com/clarion_journal_of_spirit/2020/08/certainty-uncertainty-and-wisdom-the-christian-tradition-ron-dart.html.

Davies, Oliver, ed. *Celtic Spirituality.* New York: Paulist, 1999.

Driscoll, Michael S., and J. Michael Joncas. *The Order of Mass: A Roman Missal Study Edition and Workbook.* Chicago: Archdiocese of Chicago Liturgy Training, 2011.

Duckworth, Angela. *Grit: The Power of Passion and Perseverance.* New York: Scribner, 2016.

Dionysius. *Dionysius the Areopagite: On the Divine Names and the Mystical Theology.* Translated by C. E. Rolt. PDF ed. Grand Rapids: Christian Classics Ethereal Library, 2000. http://www.ccel.org/ccel/rolt/dionysius.html.

Enns, Peter. *The Sin of Certainty: Why God Desires Our Trust More than Our "Correct" Beliefs.* New York: HarperOne, 2016

Erickson, Millard J. *Introducing Christian Doctrine.* Edited by L. Arnold Hustad. Grand Rapids: Baker Academic, 2004.

Eusebius. *Church History.* In *A Select Library of Nicene and Post-Nicene Fathers of the Christian Church*, 2nd series, edited by Philip Schaff and Henry Wace, vol. 1. Grand Rapids: Eerdmans, 1991.

Evarestus. *The Martyrdom of Polycarp.* In *The Apostolic Fathers: Early Christian Writings*, translated by Maxwell Staniforth and Andrew Louth, 123–35. New York, Penguin: 1968.

Freeman, Andy, and Pete Greig. *Punk Monk: New Monasticism and the Ancient Art of Breathing.* Ventura, CA: Regal, 2007.

French, R. M., trans. *The Way of the Pilgrim; and, The Pilgrim Continues His Way.* New York: Quality Paperback, 1998.

Greig, Peter. *Dirty Glory: Go Where Your Best Prayers Take You.* Colorado Springs, CO: NavPress, 2016.

Grenz, Stanley, and John Franke. *Beyond Foundationalism: Shaping Theology in a Postmodern Context.* Louisville: Westminster John Knox, 2001.

Hesychios the Priest. *On Watchfulness and Holiness.* In *The Philokalia: The Complete Text*, compiled by Nikodimos of the Holy Mountain and Makarios of Corinth, translated and edited by G. E. H. Palmer, Philip Sherrard, and Kallistos Ware, 1:162–98. London: Faber, 1979.

Hinlicky, Paul R. *Beloved Community: Critical Dogmatics after Christendom.* Grand Rapids: Eerdmans, 2015.

Bibliography

Hopping, Joshua S. *The Here and Not Yet: What Is Kingdom Theology and Why Does It Matter?* Ladysmith, South Africa: Vineyard International, 2017.

Howard, Evan B. *The Brazos Introduction to Christian Spirituality.* Grand Rapids: Brazos, 2008.

Hunter, George, III. *The Celtic Way of Evangelism: How Christianity Can Reach the West—Again.* Nashville: Abingdon, 2000.

Ignatius. *The Epistle to the Romans.* In *The Apostolic Fathers: Early Christian Writings*, translated by Maxwell Staniforth and Andrew Louth, 83–89. New York: Penguin, 1968.

John of the Cross. *The Dark Night of the Soul.* Translated by Gabriela Cunninghame Graham. New York: Barnes and Noble, 2005.

Johnston, William, ed. *The Cloud of Unknowing.* New York: Doubleday, 1996.

Kempis, Thomas à. *The Imitation of Christ.* Peabody, MA: Hendrickson, 2008.

Ladd, George Eldon. *The Gospel of the Kingdom: Scriptural Studies in the Kingdom of God.* Grand Rapids: Eerdmans, 1959.

Lewis, C. S. *Mere Christianity.* New York: Touchstone, 1996.

Louth, Andrew. *Discerning the Mystery: An Essay on the Nature of Theology.* Oxford: Clarendon, 1990.

———. *Maximus the Confessor.* New York: Routledge, 1996.

Markides, Kyriacos C. *Gifts of the Desert: The Forgotten Path of Christian Spirituality.* New York: Doubleday, 2005.

Mark the Ascetic. *On the Spiritual Law: Two Hundred Texts.* In *The Philokalia: The Complete Text*, compiled by Nikodimos of the Holy Mountain and Makarios of Corinth, translated and edited by G. E. H. Palmer, Philip Sherrard, and Kallistos Ware, 1:110–24. London: Faber, 1979.

———. *On Those Who Think They Are Made Righteous by Works: Two Hundred and Twenty-Six Texts.* In *The Philokalia: The Complete Text*, compiled by Nikodimos of the Holy Mountain and Makarios of Corinth, translated and edited by G. E. H. Palmer, Philip Sherrard, and Kallistos Ware, 1:125–46. London: Faber, 1979.

Maximos the Confessor. *Four Hundred Texts on Love.* In *The Philokalia: The Complete Text*, compiled by Nikodimos of the Holy Mountain and Makarios of Corinth, translated and edited by G. E. H. Palmer, Philip Sherrard, and Kallistos Ware, 2:52–113. London: Faber, 1982.

———. *Two Hundred Texts on Theology and the Incarnation Dispensation of the Son of God.* In *The Philokalia: The Complete Text*, compiled by Nikodimos of the Holy Mountain and Makarios of Corinth, translated and edited by G. E. H. Palmer, Philip Sherrard, and Kallistos Ware, 2:114–63. London: Faber, 1982.

———. *Various Texts on Theology, the Divine Economy, and Virtue and Vice.* In *The Philokalia: The Complete Text*, compiled by Nikodimos of the Holy Mountain and Makarios of Corinth, translated and edited by G. E. H. Palmer, Philip Sherrard, and Kallistos Ware, 2:164–284. London: Faber, 1982.

Medearis, Carl. *Speaking of Jesus: The Art of Not-Evangelism.* Colorado Springs, CO: David C. Cook, 2011.

Bibliography

Miller, Calvin. *The Path of Celtic Prayer: An Ancient Way to Everyday Job*. Downers Grove, IL: InterVarsity, 2007.

Mulholland, M. Robert. *Invitation to a Journey: A Road Map for Spiritual Formation*. Downers Grove, IL: InterVarsity, 2016.

Neilos the Ascetic. *Ascetic Discourse*. In *The Philokalia: The Complete Text*, compiled by Nikodimos of the Holy Mountain and Makarios of Corinth, translated and edited by G. E. H. Palmer, Philip Sherrard, and Kallistos Ware, 1:200–250. London: Faber, 1979.

Nikodimos of the Holy Mountain, and Makarios of Corinth, compilers. *The Philokalia: The Complete Text*. Translated and edited by G. E. H. Palmer, Philip Sherrard, and Kallistos Ware. Vols. 1–3. London: Faber, 1979–1986.

Nouwen, Henri. *Turn My Mourning into Dancing: Finding Hope in Hard Times*. Nashville: Thomas Nelson, 2001.

Olson, Roger E. *The Story of Christian Theology: Twenty Centuries of Tradition and Reform*. Downers Grove, IL: InterVarsity, 1999.

Perschbacher, Wesley J. *The New Analytical Greek Lexicon*. Peabody, MA: Hendrickson, 1990.

Peterson, Eugene. *A Long Obedience in the Same Direction: Discipleship in an Instant Society*. Downers Grove, IL: InterVarsity, 2000.

Ponsonby, Simon. *More: How You Can Have More of the Spirit When You Already Have Everything in Christ*. Kindle ebook ed. Colorado Springs, CO: David C. Cook, 2009.

Pseudo-Dionysius. *Dionysius the Areopagite: On the Divine Names and the Mystical Theology*. Translated by C. E. Rolt. PDF ed. Grand Rapids: Christian Classics Ethereal Library, 2000. http://www.ccel.org/ccel/rolt/dionysius.html.

Rollins, Peter. *How (Not) to Speak of God*. Brewster, MA: Paraclete, 2006.

———. *Insurrection: To Believe Is Human; To Doubt, Divine*. New York: Howard, 2011.

Rush, Alfred C. "Spiritual Martyrdom in St. Gregory the Great." *Theological Studies* 23/4 (1962) 569–89. http://cdn.theologicalstudies.net/23/23.4/23.4.2.pdf.

Sittser, Gerald L. *Water from a Deep Well: Christian Spirituality from Early Martyrs to Modern Missionaries*. Downers Grove, IL: InterVarsity, 2007.

Smith, James K. A. *Desiring the Kingdom: Worship, Worldview, and Cultural Formation*. Grand Rapids: Baker Academic, 2009.

———. *Who's Afraid of Post-Modernism?: Taking Derrida, Lyotard, and Foucault to Church*. Grand Rapids: Baker Academic, 2006.

Staniforth, Maxwell, and Andrew Louth, trans. *The Apostolic Fathers: Early Christian Writings*. New York, Penguin: 1968.

Stovell, Beth M. "Love One Another and Love the World: The Love Command and Jewish Ethics in the Johannine Community." In *Christian Origins and the Establishment of the Early Jesus Movement*, edited by Stanley E. Porter and Andrew W. Pitts, 426–58. Boston: Brill, 2018.

Bibliography

Street, R. Alan. *Heaven on Earth: Experiencing the Kingdom of God in the Here and Now.* Eugene, OR: Harvest House, 2013.

Ten Boom, Corrie. *Jesus Is Victor.* Grand Rapids: Revell, 1985.

Teresa of Avila. *The Life of St. Teresa of Avila.* Translated by David Lewis. New York: Cosimo, 2011.

Thomas, Dylan. *The Poems of Dylan Thomas.* Edited by Daniel Jones. New York: New Directions, 2003.

Thomas, Gary. *Sacred Pathways: Discovering Your Soul's Path to God.* Grand Rapids: Zondervan, 1996.

Tolkien, J. R. R. *The Hobbit: Or There and Back and Again.* New York: Houghton Mifflin Harcourt, 2001.

Waddell, Helen, ed. *The Desert Fathers.* New York: Vintage, 1998.

Ware, Kallistos. *The Orthodox Way.* Crestwood, NY: St. Vladimir's Seminary Press, 1995.

Watson, Williams. *The Poems of William Watson.* Edited by John A. Spender. Vol. 1. New York: John Lane, 1905.

Wicks, Robert J. *The Inner Life of the Counselor.* Hoboken, NJ: Wiley, 2012.

Williams, Don. *Start Here: Kingdom Essentials for Christians.* Ventura, CA: Regal, 2006.

Williams, Rick. *Uncomfortable Growth.* Lexington, KY: CreateSpace, 2015.

Wilson, Ken. *Jesus Brand Spirituality: He Wants His Religion Back.* Nashville: Thomas Nelson, 2008.

Wright, N. T. *Simply Jesus: A New Vision of Who He Was, What He Did, and Why He Matters.* New York: HaperOne, 2011.

Zahnd, Brian. *A Farewell to Mars: An Evangelical Pastor's Journey toward the Biblical Gospel of Peace.* Colorado Springs, CO: David C. Cook, 2014.

———. *Water to Wine: Some of My Story.* Kindle ebook ed. Middletown, DE: Spello, 2016.

www.ingramcontent.com/pod-product-compliance
Lightning Source LLC
Chambersburg PA
CBHW070459090426
42735CB00012B/2624